T0209971

MORE
than a Leopard

though a leopard cannot change its spots,
you can reset your inner self

MICHAEL J. PARKYN

WESTBOW
PRESS®
A DIVISION OF THOMAS NELSON
& ZONDERVAN

WestBow Press books may be ordered through
booksellers or by contacting:

WestBow Press
A Division of Thomas Nelson & Zondervan
1663 Liberty Drive
Bloomington, IN 47403
www.westbowpress.com
844-714-3454

ISBN: 978-1-6642-8595-8 (sc)
ISBN: 978-1-6642-8596-5 (hc)
ISBN: 978-1-6642-8594-1 (e)

Library of Congress Control Number: 2022922476

Print information available on the last page.

WestBow Press rev. date: 01/17/2023

Contents

Foreword

By Kenneth Lim, MD PhD MPhil FASN

Our inner health is perhaps one of the most important dimensions of well-being. However, so many of us are victims to suffering, injustice or hardships that so easily tears the fragile reality of the human heart. We are living in a world that is in crisis today, from geopolitical failures to growing injustice that confronts us all. The truth is that even as members of a civil society, one can never be fully shielded from external influences that risk corroding the core of who we are. In the 2020 National Survey on Drug Use and Health (NSDUH) by the United States (US) Substance Abuse and Mental Health Services Administration (SAMHSA), it was found that a staggering one in five adults in the US live with a mental illness. That equates to approximately 52.9 million adults aged 18 or older in the US suffering from some form of mental illness. Whether issues of mental health stem from external influences or biological (organic) causes, these are conditions that so clearly assault our inner health that is far greater than just the construct of the mind. An assault to our inner health steals away our freedom to live fully.

Perhaps, the truth of the matter is that all of the faculties or dimensions that form our inner health, from our subconscious to our spirit, risk suffering in silence in the face of adversity if not appropriately tended to. The consequences could be far reaching, involving the development of an unhealthy self-image and negatively shaping the way we feel. We risk forming unhealthy interactions with other people and reactions to the world around us. Moreover, the very core of who we are could be affected, which would be a crime against our well-being and God-ordained design. If so, to neglect the faculties that form our inner health would perhaps be a sweeping failure to our personal care. Those who struggle each grinding hour with mental illness, the desire to overcome hurt or issues of the heart who have yet to see breakthrough, or even those who are afraid to seek help are not a forgotten population. The daily struggle with unhealthy expressions of a bleeding inner self is human suffering of pandemic proportions in need of change. The promotion of human welfare or humanitarianism in its purest and most subtle form, is perhaps the right to fight for the principles of justice to relieve human suffering that is not solely confined to places of war, conflict or violence, but to our inner world.

The ability for one to transform and mend the tears of our inner health challenges the paradigm that life or aging is merely a passive, inevitable process of deteriorating organ function, including that of the mind. The assertion that one can change is so central to the dignity of inner health and to those who often suffer silently. It is one that can be so profoundly impactful when it meets people in situations of crisis. This is a topic that I believe would resonate so deeply with many readers. Importantly, it is one that transcends the divides of ethnic, racial, cultural, theological and denominational lines. It should be noted that wholeness is not an undefined status of inner health, nor is it one that has an arbitrary endpoint. Rather, one could define it as our continuing response to the Creator's love and His conforming power to transform us into His likeness. The Bible reveals that "if anyone is in Christ, the new creation has come. The old has gone, the new is here!" (2 Corinthians 5 v 17, NIV). The pathway to wholeness aims to transform one into the Creator's solution, even in the midst of a society that could be profoundly suffering. The narrative and experience of how one can journey into wholeness and to become a new creation is a book that the world so desperately needs today.

I can think of no one more fitting than Michael J. Parkyn to tackle this important topic! Gripped by a vision to mobilize a generation of people into a life of freedom and wholeness, Michael so graciously shares his story and his life-changing secrets to freedom discovered over his 30-year journey in pursuit of wholeness. Born in England, at the age of 23 he had an unexpected spiritual awakening at an inspirational rock concert in London, which propelled him onto a radically new direction in life. He then moved to South Africa in 1988 where he completed ministry training, later receiving ordination to leadership with Church of the Nations (COTN) in 1991. In South Africa, he met his lovely wife Heather and together, they have since served in four different continents (Europe, Africa, North and South America). His historical experiences have profoundly shaped him to become a globally minded visionary, with a heart to see humanity restored through personal breakthrough in our generation today.

Michael has served in various leadership roles both corporately as a director, and in ministry as church planter, pastor and trainer, and as an influencer through his Maxwell Leadership Team Certification (by John C. Maxwell). Notably, he also served as the former Operations Manager and UK Outreach Leader for Derek Prince Ministries—UK. These roles have acquainted him with both the joys and hardships that come with leading others, and the personal struggles that come with life in itself! And this is precisely why the message of this book is powerful—because all his years of challenges, hardships, path of discovery, and resulting transformative message was lived and refined for decades, long before it was written. Michael lays down principles and practices that can change your life and the world around you. This book invites you to journey into the unknown. This journey is one that is by no means passive and by no means a contented action. This book will provoke, challenge your existing paradigms, and help you to go deep beneath-the-surface to bring lasting transformation. This journey will edify your soul and help you implement truths in replacement of false beliefs. It will be most impactful to those who are willing to read it thoughtfully and prayerfully, to those who are willing to exercise the power of humility, who dare to transcend the equations of science and logic, and to those who dare to dream of reaching new frontiers in life. Moreover, this book provides one of the most important invitations one can receive, that is, to enter into a deeper and wider relationship with Jesus.

Today, Michael and Heather are part of the International House of Prayer in Kansas City (IHOPKC). They are strategically positioned to positively impact a generation and take forward their mission to help others experience wholeness, for which they attract a global audience. The world needs transformed people who live in a place of wholeness. This is because transformed people made whole in the likeness of Christ live out their true God-ordained destiny! They are people who are positioned to make the greatest impact in our world. Beyond the gripping message of this first book, the world now eagerly awaits the next installment.

Dr. Ken Lim, MD PhD MPhil FASN is an American Physician-Scientist, Nephrologist, Entrepreneur and Public Figure. He holds Professorships at the Indiana University School of Medicine and was formerly Faculty Member at Harvard Medical School and Attending Physician at The Massachusetts General Hospital. He has served as strategic advisor or consultant to leaders from diverse sectors, he has held offices of leadership on numerous corporate and non-profit boards and has appeared on various television and media programs. In 2022, he was named by the Indianapolis Business Journal to the Forty Under 40 list of most influential young leaders.

Acknowledgments

This book has been a long while in the incubator. It carries years of exploring, growing, and progressing, as I sought personal inner freedom and wholeness.

No one has stood by me, supportive, patient, gracious, encouraging (I could list a dozen more positive adjectives) like my "gift from God" wife, Heather. She is the best! Without her, I'm not sure where I'd be, but you likely wouldn't have this book in your hand today.

Alongside Heather, there have been a group of folk who supported my mission to get this content into print: Bonny, Hannah, Ken, Mikaela, Phil, and Sonnie. Thank you for your support and participation in the review of the content. I appreciate you all; your lives inspire me.

And thank you, Eric Schroeder at WestBow Press. This book delves into dealing with false or limiting beliefs that shape us. There was a danger that my own such beliefs might have kept this book in the "one day maybe" category. Your first phone call, showing such support and encouragement, smashed that. I will be forever grateful.

Finally, I have been immensely encouraged and energized by our loving Creator. His mercies are truly new every morning. Knowing Him as Father has changed and shaped me. All of this is intended for His renown.

Glossary

There are several key phrases and terms that are used often in this book. They are fundamental to understanding the text. Here they are:

1. Subconscious. This is an inner part of our being we are not conscious of. However, it appears to have significant influence on our behavior and life experiences. Although we cannot see this consciously, we can identify its condition somewhat by observing outward, conscious symptoms. There are two components of the subconscious that we discuss extensively:
   a. Self-Image: An inner picture of how we see ourselves, formed mostly by life experiences and our own personal beliefs.
   b. Auto-pilot System (APS). This is a phrase used to describe an engineering-type automatic mechanism, that actively functions within the subconscious to influence our behavior. It operates to steer our behavior or life experiences in a way that will match our self-image. It is similar to how a guided missile is fixed on a target and constantly updates its progress to make sure it hits the target. In the case of our lives, the target is our self-image.
2. Intentional Calmness. This is a technique that allows us to temporarily de-activate the APS, so that the self-image can be updated or reshaped.

3. Visualization. This technique uses the imagination to reshape our self-image without the need for new, corrective life experiences.
4. Conscious Realignment. This is where we intentionally engage our conscious faculties to pursue the same objectives being adopted in the re-shaping of our self-image. It also includes adopting a set of personal beliefs we intentionally develop, targeted use of words, and the application of practical faith.
5. New Spirit. This is the result of a creative act by the Creator, at our invitation. A new human spirit is created within us, formed in purity, and free from corruption. Receiving this new spirit brings us into a new creation reality and provides us with a direct basis to reshape our self-image into wholeness.
6. Dianoia. This is a Greek word used in the Bible that has been taken in this book to mean the subconscious. This is explained in chapter 12 and expounded upon further in the subsequent chapters.

Welcome

Collins Dictionary describes the *leopard cannot change its spots* idiom this way:

> "If you say that a leopard cannot change its spots, you mean that people or things are not able to change their basic characteristics, especially when you are critical of those characteristics."[i]

This book exists to refute this idea. We can change our basic characteristics. We do not have to stay as we are. This is a breath of fresh air to people feeling stuck in life, wishing things could change. They can change. You can literally reset your inner self.

My book is intentionally brief and, hopefully, fairly easy to read. We are going to dive into some pretty deep concepts, but my goal is to make them as simple to grasp as possible.

Our subject includes certain aspects of mental health, an area society has been acknowledging more and more in recent years, which is a good thing. This book is written around my own story and path of discovery, which has led me into some accelerated growth towards wholeness. I am in the best place I have ever been in, from a mental health perspective. But the book is actually about more than just mental health in the normal sense and moves us into what I might call inner health. There is more to who we are inside than just the mental aspect; we are more than just a mind.

I invite you to take this journey into discovering more

about yourself and learning how you can function closer to your best. This is a book about our inner person. And of course that is complex. There are a lot of moving parts, and it is surprising to me that many of us just storm through life, not giving much thought to what is going on inside. Because of that, we are often just living obliviously in the consequences of what is in there, more than with any particular intentionality. I hope I can help shift that for you. Things really can change for the good, and you can take back control.

It helps if you approach the content with at least a partly open mind. Most of the core ideas came as a big surprise to me when I found them, and I was delighted to experience a lot of progress quite quickly. The best thing is, wherever you are on your journey through life, you can start right where you are.

Do you feel like you might need some kind of inner reset? A bit like an electronic device that isn't working right? Just hit the reset button, or disconnect the power and restart. Most of us are aware that we have been shaped by past circumstances, by our experiences, and by the culture that surrounds us. There have been hurts, mistakes made, maybe a wrong turn here or there. Or even just a blandness in life, like something is missing. The idea of being able to reset our inner self might sound appealing.

Today, as I reflect on significant breakthroughs I made around my personal wholeness and well-being, I definitely discovered some keys. Erroneously, for years, I held to the fear-founded view that soul issues like the subconscious are in opposition to conventional (Christian) spiritual reality. I have found that nothing could be further from the truth. I have found most progress where I can reconcile the two, where inner harmony works towards wholeness. I have found I need to engage both the helpful insights of psychology *and* the spirituality.

This is my story, and my path of discovery into freedom and the pursuit of wholeness. I invite you to explore with me, as I retrace my steps, sharing some of the biggest lessons I have learned along the way.

Part 1

The Normal Human Life: Who Are We?

What a joy it is to celebrate diversity and uniqueness. The human race is so varied, made up of many awesomely unique individuals, so even using the term "normal human life" may seem highly presumptuous. What do I mean by the normal human life? I'm thinking of our humanness. We all actually do have a lot in common. In very broad, simple terms, we all have a physical body and an inner person. We put a lot of emphasis on the outward and physical, and society is obsessed with it: appearance, ethnicity, height, weight, age, fitness, hair, muscles, manicures, and more.

All this has its place, but that is not the focus of this book. I want us to think about and look at our inner faculties. Of course, this is a bit harder to do, because they are in the unseen realm. So we have to make observations, draw conclusions, and pull evidence together through scientific study, including psychology. In my experience, the Bible has some powerful things to say about who we are too, but that will be for later in the book.

Chapter 1

Inner Faculties

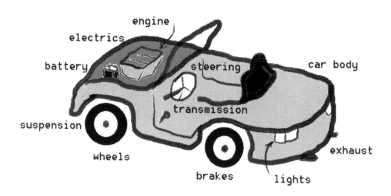

Our inner person has many faculties. I'm not trying to do a thorough technical or psychological analysis here; I am not qualified to do that. Rather, I just want to create a framework for our journey to get us on the same general page.

We are all familiar with the five physical senses: sight, smell, taste, touch, and hearing. I'm not really concerned so much with those here, except to acknowledge they exist. It's an easy on-ramp to discovering our common normal, irrespective of ethnicity, gender identity, politics, or religious persuasion.

The next layer is a bit deeper, and it is where a lot of who we are seems to happen. Our minds (thinking), will (choosing), and emotions (feeling) are the big three. Some people refer to these collectively as the soul, although that might be a bit oversimplistic. For certain, different people express their personality through the greater or lesser dominance of one or more of these three. And when it comes to personality, our common ground is only that we all have one. Each one of us has our own personality.

It is interesting how greater dominance of one or more of these basic faculties can shape our personality. For example, we've all met people who seem headstrong or academic. Perhaps they are deep thinkers, rational, logical. They operate significantly in the realm of the mind. But that doesn't necessarily mean they have control over their minds. Perhaps they are plagued by thoughts they'd rather not have. A lot of Western emphasis is concerned with developing the mind, centered on the acquisition of knowledge and the ability to think. There are lots of techniques on how to improve this and many self-help books on the topic.

You can probably think of someone you know who is strong-willed. Such people can seem difficult, especially if you, too, are strong-willed, so that interactions sometimes feel more like a clash. But equally, two strong-willed people working together with a common purpose can be hugely productive. Other aspects of being somewhat dominated by our will might include being dogmatic, insistent, demanding, determined, intentional, or proactive. Although strong-willed people can be the most dynamic and influential, they can also get trapped in habits and behavioral patterns that they might prefer weren't so dominant.

What of the emotional type? We all have emotions, but people whose emotions are the dominant faculty can become the center of drama very quickly. Perhaps there are mood swings or bursts of enthusiasm, joy, or spontaneity. They may feel depressed, withdrawn, or heavy. Emotionally driven people can affect the atmosphere in a room. By definition, the more emotional among us are driven very much by what they feel.

I mention these briefly just so we recognize we all have these three main faculties, and the degree to which they operate affects who we are and who others perceive us to be. Making ourselves the unaware slaves of these core faculties can shape our lives significantly. We would do well to take steps to manage them and learn to use them for positive outcomes. Yet it seems to be a commonly held belief that we can't do much about all this. We say, "That's just the way I am."

At the heart of this book is my intention to challenge that idea and help us understand that we do not have to stay the way we are. We can change.

Beyond the immediate big three faculties of thinking, choosing, and feeling are some underlying deeper levels, like motivation, conscience, understanding, memory, passions, sex drive, beliefs, and faith. These are the heartier parts of our inner nature and likely where our values sit. Each of these influences the three main faculties already described, and those three faculties are the tools of expression of the deeper characteristics of who we are.

What motivates you? For many of us, it might be quite hard to answer that. What is that thing inside you that determines your priorities? Of similar mystery is perhaps the role of the conscience and the way it is shaped. Generally, the conscience is understood to be some kind of moral inner compass, able to nudge us if we are heading in some wrong or bad direction. And, conversely, it prompts us toward a right or good one. But who defines the standards for the conscience? Often these come from outside ourselves, dictated by parents, culture, society, and popular norms. Every generation also has its time for kicking against those and redefining the framework our conscience must adopt. For some, the very thought of being shaped by culture is itself aggravating. In fact, protecting their right to be an individual and not conform becomes the key driver of everything.

Did I say this is complex? It is, for sure.

On my journey, I did not give too much attention to finding out how these inner faculties work. In my spiritual progression, I knew my mind somehow needed to be trained to think good thoughts, and my will aligned in obedience to moral, ethical, and godly standards. Emotions? I guess they needed to be controlled, kept in line. It troubled me that personal progress in this sense felt more like constraint than freedom. And it was a constant inner battle, where it seemed the things I knew I should do or be like were opposed somehow—even from within myself.

This seemed rather typical and in line with the status quo, so I just accepted that for years. I was always looking for ways to grow, though, and often led groups where I was exposed to other peoples' challenges and needs too. So there has been steady progress in various ways and a sense of continual learning. But then I came across the subconscious realm, and understanding this has led to unprecedented and accelerated growth.

Perhaps you explored that realm yourself before, but for me, it was new. For many people I come across, there is not much understanding of what this is. The subconscious seems pretty mystical, untouchable, and unknown. Of course it is. If we were conscious of it, it would no longer be subconscious. But just because it is not readily known or recognizable does not mean it is not real. My journey into the subconscious realm made a very big impact on me, and this will be the subject of our next chapter.

Chapter 2

Discover the Subconscious

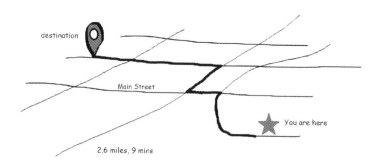

destination

Main Street

You are here

2.6 miles, 9 mins

I f you have given time and effort in the past to working on developing your better-known conscious inner faculties I named in chapter 1, you will doubtless have gained some tangible benefit. For me, in my twenties, I made a dive into the possibility of being changed for the better. There are always outside influences and influencers that will contribute to that, but I slowly became aware that I, too, could do something to help, more intentionally. By my early forties, I had embraced the value of coaching and mentoring, and I sought to be coached and mentored as well as to develop in ways that would allow me to be able to help others too.

The idea that we can change for the good by our own choice and intention is actually quite a glorious prospect. Before I started to become aware of the possibilities and benefits, I was very much just a product of things beyond my control. For example, I had no say in when or where I was born, the family I found myself in, or the culture and society that surrounded me. I became just another output of the big machine.

One conscious step I took to heart was the notion that what comes into my inner being could influence me, especially things I see or hear. I remember a time when a group of us, becoming aware of this, referenced the "eye gate" and the "ear gate." I liken it also to a garden, where seeds blowing in the wind may fall and nestle into the soil. Other seeds might be planted more intentionally. The result is that they all, potentially at least, grow to make a statement in the garden and become a crop. Of course, the fruit matches the plant, which arises from a specific seed. We don't get tomatoes from planting sunflowers.

So my quest was to be careful of what entered through those two big gates—the eyes and the ears. Possibly because of this, I've not been a big movie watcher, but scenes including violence, profanity, or immorality would immediately make me jump up to slam the gate shut and block the seeds. I concluded it is a lot easier to keep seeds out than to try to deal with what they grow into after the event.

Over time, I also developed a clearer sense of my core values, what matters to me, and how I want to live. I was determined to create a positive framework, to hopefully flourish and even make a worthwhile contribution to others, whether specific individuals or even wider society. That might sound pretentious, but it seemed to me that all of us must be here for a reason. Surely we have purpose?

It reminds me of something a friend said about my father at his funeral. Dad had lived a decent amount of time and passed at the age of eighty-eight. My friend described him simply as "a good man." Now, how we judge the rightness of that statement would need another book, but in really basic terms, I guess that's what I was after: to be a good man. If you want to drill down a bit, for me as a family man, it meant being a good husband, a good dad, a good neighbor, and so forth. Some kind of positive influence. I was pretty satisfied with this framework and basic philosophy for life, and I was quietly proud of some noticeable progress. Not that I had made it yet, of course, but still.

But there was a troubling undercurrent. There seemed to be some things I just wasn't able to access or intentionally improve. Deciding to become tidier, not leave dirty clothes lying around, or not leave used dishes unwashed all seemed doable. It's just a choice. But changing my feelings or my ability to express myself or connect in certain ways wasn't as easy. How do you begin to adjust those kinds of things? Another troubling tendency I noticed was how I was often making progress in a certain area, only to slip back and struggle to maintain progress. Examples included trying to become more confident or developing a willingness to take on leadership roles, or even planning to write a book. It was all too common that I would enjoy some success, only to find a tendency to slip back again.

At times, it felt like the term "dealing with my demons" was perhaps more than just an idiom. I even addressed that in the past by actively trying to practice a mild form of self-exorcism, as explained in a self-help book someone had given me. What if I could just cast out my weaknesses and failings? But it didn't seem to change anything for me.

(Don't get me wrong, there can be demon-related issues, and properly handled deliverance of demons definitely has its place.) I concluded that, at that time, I probably just needed to apply even more self-discipline to my life.

But then my breakthrough came. When I heard entrepreneur and inspirational trainer Paul Martinelli mention how Maxwell Maltz's book *Psycho Cybernetics*[ii] had influenced him so positively, I decided I should check it out for myself. I had to face down some strong inner convictions against even reading that book, because the title sounded very off on my value system, not that I had a clue what it meant; it just sounded a bit like what some people might call new age or weird. In my background, psycho meant weird. And as for cybernetics? I'd never heard of that word.

Titles can be off-putting. The term "cybernetics" comes from the Greek word *kybernētēs* and carries the idea of a ship's captain steering their ship successfully into port.[iii] *Psycho* just means "inner soul." So Dr. Maltz's book is a study on how we can steer our inner life towards desired behavior goals (at least that's my approximate interpretation). The piece I was most impacted by was the idea that we have a subconscious part of us that includes what Maltz calls a "servo-mechanism."[iv]

"Servo-mechanism" is an engineering term for "a device or system that corrects the performance of a mechanism by means of an error-sensing feedback."[v] This works to help a device meet its objectives or hit its target. According to *Science Direct*, a servo mechanism typically includes three parts. First, it has a "sensor" that detects any error between the "desired target" and the actual current status or direction. Second, it has a "controller" that then directs any necessary "corrective" adjustment on the device direction, speed, position, and so on. Third, it has a "feedback" connection that monitors the impact of the change made.[vi] One example of such a system is that used in a guided missile. The missile is set on a target but then relies on constant feedback and adjustment, to allow it to correct course, as needed to hit the target.

The concept I grasped is that the mechanism in our

subconscious automatically directs the course of our lives towards fulfilment of our inner goals and beliefs. As I worked to understand this, I found this inner mechanism is like a powerful inner driver that actually shapes our life experience. It cannot be fooled; it just works mechanically and automatically with whatever target it is given. And here is the vital key: That inner target is defined by our own inner self-image. Our self-image is basically how we see ourselves, and what is contained in our core inner beliefs. This inner self-image is formed through life experiences, our value systems, etc., and in some ways is a kind of passive inner faculty itself.

The significance of the inner mechanism is that it works to enforce, or outwork, whatever it sees in the self-image. If we have behavior that is contrary, it actually works to correct that, to drive our behavior back towards whatever the self-image contains. So if my self-image is one of shyness, the mechanism reacts against me trying to be too self-confident and steers me back towards being shy. If my self-image is one of being a high achiever, the mechanism reacts against me being sloppy or half-hearted, and motivates me to push harder. Literally, whatever is in that self-image is what this mechanism works to enforce.

If my self-image is healthy, the system automatically works in me to guide me in a way that matches that, and things go well. But if I have a poor or damaged self-image for some reason, the mechanism can do nothing else but guide my life from that position. In this way, I can find myself stuck in a rut, or life pattern, that is hard to break. In many ways, the inner servo-mechanism seems to embrace a similar role to an auto-pilot system on a plane or vehicle. For simplicity, from this point, I will simply call this inner servo-mechanism our auto-pilot system, or APS. I will be referencing the APS a lot through this book. That is because discovering it, and finding out how it works, has been a huge part of my journey into freedom and greater inner health.

The APS is entirely subconscious. We are not aware of it working. The self-image it targets is also entirely subconscious, so we don't know what the APS is trying to comply with. We operate in the conscious realm. Our thoughts, feelings, choices, our five physical senses, are all in our awareness. They are conscious. For years, all of my pursuits towards growth or wholeness were entirely in the conscious realm. I didn't know there was such a tangible thing in the subconscious as a self-image and an auto-pilot system.

So here is an important question I had to ask myself: What if my self-image is different from my conscious focus? What if the APS is working contrary to my conscious faculties? That variance will unavoidably lead to inner conflict, and that had been my story. I had never understood that this was happening. The more I tried harder consciously, set specific goals, or resolved to improve myself in some way, the greater the conflict became. Because my working harder was in the conscious realm, and I wasn't doing anything to change the inner self-image to align with that. So the APS was pushing me towards fulfilling something different from what I was trying to achieve consciously. What a discovery this was.

I am a person of faith, and one thing I picked up in my pursuit of spiritual things was an all-too-common awareness of falling short. Some sectors of the religious community are quick to tell us that we are all sinners, unworthy, undeserving. If I agree with that and own it as an inner belief, my self-image becomes shaped like that. That's who I am. Do you know what that means? It means the APS is actively operating to keep my behavior and life experience in line with falling short. And yet in my conscious mind, choices, and desires, I am trying to be that good man. What inner conflict. What frustration.

Going beyond the general or religious, each of us is impacted by things we hear about ourselves (especially in formative years) and also things that happened to us. Perhaps you were told you'd never achieve anything great. Or you experienced something embarrassing or humiliating. Or latched on to something as true when it wasn't, so you believe a lie. Perhaps you have a poor profile on social media that makes you feel inferior. Our self-image is being shaped and formed constantly by everything around us and by our internal responses to our experiences.

I once heard of someone who was asked to say a few words publicly, but they froze up, blushed, and felt a failure. It seems like an inner belief or image was established right then in their self-image, where they were quietly determined that such an experience would never happen to them again. Talking in public became difficult, and any excuse possible was used to avoid having to. Years later, when the need arose to speak in a meeting at work, even though they didn't consciously recall that bad experience from before, their APS worked against them, with a protective objective, making them unable to fulfil well what they needed to do.

Of course, our APS isn't supposed to make things go badly for us. Rather, it is there to help us fulfil our abilities, our dreams, and our desires. Maybe to compose music, write code, run a successful business, or be a great mom, dad, or friend. But if our self-image within is not consistent with doing well in those ways, or our inner beliefs are contrary, our APS will steer us in a way that hinders rather than fulfils those desires.

For years, I had no idea this was happening within me. Having discovered it, I wondered, could this be an explanation for my bursts of progress instigated by my conscious efforts, followed by some relapse or slipping back? Perhaps it could explain my complete inability to even access important parts of me? It left me with a burning question: What was the condition of my self-image? How had my experiences shaped it, and what was the target my APS was set to hit? And maybe a bigger question was, is there any way I can change that target? How can I access and change my self-image?

On my own faith journey, it seemed I had some extra baggage to cope with too. Far from helping the situation, I found that religion can seriously hinder us in our pursuit of personal freedom and wholeness. Maybe some readers can relate. Not only was there the failure mentality (I'm always going to fall short), but also, I didn't remember seeing anything about a subconscious realm or APS in the pages of the Bible. I knew I would feel a lot happier pursuing this new realm further if there was at least some mention of it, so I went to searching. And do you know what I found? The subconscious is in the Bible. (If this is important to you, feel free to jump ahead to chapter 12 quickly, where I explain how and where I found this. Then come back and continue here.)

But do you know what? Knowing this is all in the Bible is helpful whether you have a personal faith or not, because it validates the whole subconscious framework from one of the oldest, most established and influential books on the planet. (It's still the top selling book of all time, according to Guinness World Records.[vii]) So this is not some quirky new fad.

Although we cannot observe either our self-image or our APS (they are both subconscious, remember), we can look for conscious symptoms that may indicate what is happening in our subconscious realm. From these, we can assess the condition of our self-image, so that we can begin to apply ways to shift it. Much of this book is on how to reset our self-image. In the next chapter, I will discuss some of those symptoms, so we can start the process of finding out what is going on in there.

Chapter 3

Symptoms of Our Inner Condition

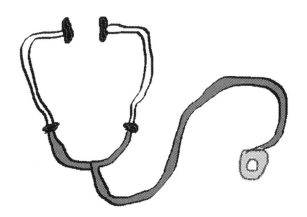

Oftentimes, medical doctors look for symptoms when trying to identify physical problems. Maybe I have a high temperature, chest pains, or headaches. Perhaps I have high blood pressure or an abnormal heart rhythm. Armed with these kinds of symptoms, medical professionals are steered towards diagnosis or towards further, deeper investigation. In the same way, we can detect symptoms that might indicate the condition of our unseen subconscious and particularly our self-image.

Although there are deeper and more meaningful life goals that we will explore later, to start with, I will keep this diagnosis simple, framing our subconscious diagnosis around how well we seem to be doing in life generally. Here are a few common symptoms that might apply when things seem to be going well:

- having a clear sense of purpose
- embracing a good sense of personal worth or value
- demonstrating a determined attitude, persevering
- having kindness and interest in others' well-being
- exhibiting general contentment
- living with self-confidence

Typically, people who exhibit the above symptoms are not striving to be somebody, but are content with their current state of progress.

Does that list describe you? If it does, or you relate to most of them, your self-image is probably in pretty good shape. Your APS is typically working with you, rather than against you.

But for many of us, there are probably some gaps or variances that might indicate otherwise. These are the kinds of characteristics that could be symptoms of a less healthy self-image:

- hopelessness
- dissatisfaction
- loneliness
- inadequacy

- inferiority
- inner anger
- antagonism
- indecisiveness
- sense of blandness
- irrational fears or panic attacks

The list could go on, but this is enough to give you the general idea. You could probably think of some of your own too. Although these are all typically negative in nature, they can all be used as positive feedback, a bit like getting sudden pain on the right side of the lower abdomen may indicate a case of appendicitis and steer us towards life-saving surgery.

I was able to identify with most of that second list at some level, especially when I took time to think through them. Let me do that briefly with you now.

Hopelessness and dissatisfaction. We all have elements of feeling hopeless or dissatisfied, as we encounter the various challenges or setbacks life throws at us. That's not abnormal and isn't immediately a symptom of a self-image problem. What we are looking for here is chronic or consistent dissatisfaction, where you might describe yourself as a dissatisfied person. For me, it wasn't as strong as being hopeless, but I could sense ongoing frustration, especially where I found myself behaving differently from what I would want or choose, or falling short on standards I set myself.

Loneliness. This is a big one. A 2021 study by Harvard[viii] found that 36 percent of all Americans—including 61 percent of young adults and 51 percent of mothers with young children—feel "serious loneliness." Again, we all have some loneliness feelings from time to time. The symptom we are looking for here is a more extended or deeper loneliness, where we feel distant from people around us. Perhaps even a kind of inner distancing from ourselves. Sometimes, loneliness can indicate that we are engaging self-protection, where isolation is considered better than repeated exposure to hurt or humiliation.

Inadequacy and inferiority. It was hard for me to admit this in myself, but in talking with others, I realize this is quite common. We may have some imagined ideal that we know we are not achieving. In my experience, this was rooted especially in the disappointment of making some progress with a certain goal, only to then fall back. It often felt like I was taking one step forwards, then two steps back. Although I didn't realize it, my expectation had become formed in that pattern, and that shaped my self-image. So even when I set out to achieve something like personal fitness, improved eating habits, or better engagement with others, it would maybe go well for a while, and then I would fall back again.

Inner anger. Inner anger is something that festers within; it's often a development of frustration or inner disappointment. At times, it can develop and emerge a bit like blowing a pressure valve. Common examples include irritability, fault-finding, and maybe gossip. In myself, I found myself being moody, critical, and self-centered. For others, perhaps it drives them towards addictions, including overworking. Sometimes, it might even turn more inward, causing physical ailments like ulcers or high blood pressure.

Antagonism. Antagonism often surfaces out of an inner sense of personal failure. Rather than facing the pain of that and dealing with it, we instead start looking for a scapegoat, or someone or something else to blame. This might be specific and personal, or just a feeling that life in general is against us. Unfortunately, someone given to antagonism doesn't come across as the most desirous person to be around, which fuels more rejection and can just strengthen the conclusion that "everyone is against me."

Indecisiveness. Indecisive people have no clear direction or sense of purpose. Or perhaps they have lots of options and just struggle to choose the right one. This symptom can be rooted in a type of perfectionism or unrealistic expectation, where we become paralyzed for fear of making the wrong decision. In my case, I saw this even in my approach to buying something like a new household appliance. I would spend hours and hours comparing different ones, nervously trying to make the right choice. I recognized within me what Elbert Hubbard said, "The greatest mistake a person can make is to be afraid of making one."[ix]

Sense of blandness. Recognizing this in myself made me sad. I found myself struggling to really enjoy things. Even things I liked seemed empty or bland. Experiences I was grateful for didn't seem to create a sense of inner happiness. Why was that? Often, we don't know. And while sometimes there is value in trying to dig back to find the cause of something, often it is enough to just recognize the symptom and start working on changing the self-image.

Irrational fears or panic attacks. Irrational fears are very common and play heavily on the conscious mind. Sometimes, they become set up in the self-image at specific moments in time, when there may be genuine reason for fear. But then they just fester within and become triggered when certain circumstances arise. Most phobias work like this. When they are triggered, they can be paralyzing, leading to the panic attack.

Do you recognize any of these traits in yourself? We all have our own traits; these are just examples.

When we realize we have these symptoms, they become indicators of the kind of self-image or set of inner beliefs the APS is targeting. The APS is an automatic system that will always look to steer our behavior in directions consistent with our self-image. Facing up to these symptoms can allow us to use them for positive progress. There are several techniques we can apply to help reset our self-image, so the APS works to hit a different target. Our life can change.

One word of warning, though: I discovered that many of

us have a tendency to fear changing. So even going through that list might lead us to conclude we are being too hard on ourselves and need to be realistic. Sometimes, we are stuck in passivity and even prefer to stay in the issue rather than face it. Sometimes, our specific problem even becomes our identity and attracts sympathy or attention from others. It becomes our comfort zone, and we decide to stay there rather than grow in our inner health. My advice would be, don't give in to that self-defeating loop. Rather, see these kinds of symptoms as something that can really help you move forward.

So now it is time to move into the exciting part. Having looked for symptoms, how do we treat the cause? Many folk, not yet aware of this inner, subconscious realm, turn to treating the symptoms in the conscious, not the cause in the subconscious. But it rarely works, at least not in the longer term. It is much better to work on reshaping the self-image rather. How do we do that? That will be the focus of part 2. See you there.

Part 2

Reshaping Our Self-Image

Hopefully by now, you have grasped a basic understanding that within each of us is this subconscious reality, our self-image. This informs an auto-pilot system (APS) that steers us towards fulfilling whatever the self-image contains. The self-image is typically formed around a set of inner beliefs that have developed and been adopted as true, through past experiences.

In the previous chapter, we looked at symptoms that reveal the likely condition of our self-image. Where we see negative symptoms, we can introduce some simple techniques that can help reshape the self-image.

Of course, this is potentially a complex subject, and I am not in a position to present a detailed technical analysis or prescribe therapy here. But there are a few simple approaches you can begin to apply that, from my experience, can help to bring some noticeable improvements. I am excited to share them with you in the coming chapters.

Chapter 4

Intentional Calmness

One Sunday morning, my wife called me from downstairs, saying, "We have a big problem in the kitchen." Having no idea what she meant, my mind jumped to what might be going on. Had a raccoon climbed in the window? Nothing that exciting. There was water coming through the ceiling. Now, you don't have to be a design professional, or an experienced contractor, to know this was not supposed to be happening. Nor to know that the immediate urgent need was to find out where the water was coming from and turn off the supply.

In our case, it wasn't a burst pipe or a leaking faucet, but rather a broken seal on the shower in the bathroom above. Water was getting behind the tile and finding its way down to the kitchen below. (Oh, the joy of older houses.) "Turn off the shower." Needless to say, this opened up an urgent remodel project that tore out old and damaged components and replaced them with new.

That's a pretty good picture of what we are trying to do here, step by step. First, turn off the shower. We need to identify what is causing the problem in our APS and neutralize it. Turn it off. Stop it producing and reproducing. And then, we need to remove damaged components in our self-image and replace them with new, better ones. The techniques I share in this part of the book will address these steps, in one way or another. In this chapter, I want to talk about how to disconnect the source.

First of all, we need to neutralize the APS or cause it to pause. There are characteristics in our self-image that will continue to be the target our APS is steering us towards fulfilling, unless we temporarily disengage it. The APS can perpetuate a vicious cycle that is difficult to get free from using just our normal conscious faculties.

As a start, what I have found helpful is distancing myself from the opinion of others or even various norms that society or religion might be trying to dictate to me. I don't need to own those. All around me, I see people who have very varied ability, standards, and personality. So I can begin by accepting my own uniqueness as a human being. I found huge relief in simply setting my goal to be me.

Then, I can set about changing my self-image and core beliefs. If I can do that, then the APS will adjust towards fulfilling that new image or belief. The APS has no moral compass itself; it has no personality. It is purely mechanical. It can work as powerfully for us as it can against us, depending on whether or not the self-image is aligned with our desired direction. But how do we change our self-image or inner beliefs?

Typically, it seems, the inner image is formed mostly through our experiences in life. If I achieve a certain success, I believe I can do it again. Conversely, if I take a knock, I reshape future expectations around that experience. Remember, this is all subconscious. None of this is something I settle on by reason or choice. But I become shaped, experience by experience. Then the APS keeps working to hit the target of the self-image. So it self-replicates or strengthens, like a rut or carved-out trail.

Now, if I manage to actively develop new experiences with different outcomes, that will definitely help reshape my inner self-image. But that is often hard to do, especially because the APS is working to fulfil the existing self-image target. And sometimes, we cannot easily create experiences that readily offset the self-image problem. What if there is some other way to access the self-image from within and change it? Like downloading a new file on my computer or getting a system upgrade on my phone?

None of us had to intentionally work to create that inner belief or self-image. It came naturally, effortlessly, just from whatever experience we went through. This presents quite a profound counter-intuitive realization. Contrary to just trying harder, working differently, or trying to force a change from my conscious realm, I realized the way to access my inner self-image, and change it, was through first becoming still, by actually practicing calmness. This is how the APS becomes disengaged or temporarily neutralized. It is in that calm state that a new inner trait can begin to be formed. This became the first new discipline I learned to apply: practicing intentional inner calmness. With this, I recognized a similar principle I knew from the Bible already, where it says simply to "be still and know that God is God" (Psalm 46:10).

I decided to try this. Rather than try to set another new conscious goal, to shift my experiences, I decided to just stop and become calm. It amazed me how impactful this was.

As a culture, we Westerners are not given to intentional calmness. Most education and training teaches something like the opposite. It is all about taking action, creating strategies, setting goals, and so on. And don't get me wrong; that is all good and helpful in the conscious realm. But we are trying here to access the subconscious, which doesn't work like that. Let me explain how I learned to practice intentional calmness. First, it is important not to equate calmness with emptiness. It is not the absence of activity, but more the presence of peace, and it's experienced as we fully engage calmness. You might like to try this:

Find a comfortable place to sit or even lie down. Then consciously relax, breathing slowly, letting go of tension. Perhaps use some calming music. This is using our conscious awareness, and it's a good start. But something shifted for me when I realized I could go deeper than this, if I learned to also engage the APS I have been talking about. What if I could set an inner target of calmness for the APS, so that it guides me towards that? This was a new realm for me. How could I do that?

The simplest way I have of explaining this is by visualization. I had always been wary of anything like that, thinking it was some kind of Eastern religion or spiritual practice I might not be comfortable exploring. It is indeed true that certain forms of spirituality have learned to engage visualization well, but that doesn't mean it is wrong or bad for the rest of us. It just means that those who practice it have learned to tap into something we have rejected or just been unaware of. Somehow, though, that Psalm 46 quote above reassured me. I felt comfortable pursuing this. I should mention briefly here that I have since discovered visualization principles much more directly and powerfully in the Bible too. I will be explaining that in a lot of detail later in the book.

But back to the task in hand. There I was, lying on my back, relaxed, breathing slowly, releasing tension. It felt good. But then I discovered that visualization would allow me to dive deeper into calmness. There are lots of ways to do this, but there is one simple technique that I found worked well for me. This was simply visualizing inner tension like air inside me, that had me blown up like a balloon. I then visualized a stopper on my thigh and simply opened it to let the air out. As I imagined my body starting to slowly deflate, all the inner tension left.

Next, I connected a real memory of a time when I was actually calm. Immediately, my APS could identify with this easily as a genuine target. It was a real experience I had. One of my favorites is remembering when I was on vacation in Florida and relaxed on an inflatable boat in the warm sun, all alone on the calm Gulf of Mexico. Recalling this, and visualizing it, allowed the APS to lead me into a level of calmness I could not achieve just consciously.

Perhaps you would like to try this. Allow yourself fifteen minutes or longer, if you have more time. Follow through the process I described, and see where you land.

Learning to intentionally practice calmness in this way was the first technique I learned for reshaping my self-image. It was also my first attempt at engaging the power of the APS, opening up an exciting prospect I had never encountered before. If the APS could engage calmness for me through visualization, why not try visualization with other goals too? Can you see what this discovery means? Intentional calmness and visualization could allow me to access my subconscious realm, regarding any aspect of my self-image, and then change it, by visualizing new experiences. I remember the feeling of incredible hope that now any aspect of my inner health could potentially be impacted for the good.

It reminded me of what the World Health Organization outlines as true health. The WHO constitution states, "Health is a state of complete physical, mental and social well-being and not merely the absence of disease or infirmity." The WHO then clarifies, "An important implication of this definition is that mental health is more than just the absence of mental disorders or disabilities. Mental health is a state of well-being in which an individual realizes his or her own abilities, can cope with the normal stresses of life, can work productively and is able to make a contribution to his or her community. Mental health is fundamental to our collective and individual ability as humans to think, emote, interact with each other, earn a living and enjoy life. On this basis, the promotion, protection and restoration of mental health can be regarded as a vital concern of individuals, communities and societies throughout the world."[x]

Chapter 5

Visualization

H opefully, you got a chance to try an intentional calmness session like I explained in the last chapter. If so, maybe this chapter will be an easy win for us. When I first visualized taking a stopper out of my thigh to let the air of inner tension out, I honestly thought, *This is just crazy; what am I doing this for?* But as I persisted, I experienced the impact. A deep sense of calmness seemed to overwhelm me. And I knew I could not have achieved that by trying to become calm consciously or by trying to just be inactive. I actually was experiencing the effect of my own APS at work. I had struggled through life, completely unaware that I even had an APS, a self-image, or a subconscious realm. Now I knew I was on to something and was determined to explore this more.

Isn't it fascinating that we humans have an in-built ability to visualize? What do you think it is there for? Much like all our inner faculties and abilities, it can be used towards corruption or misuse, and for sure society has examples of that all around us. How about exploring the idea that it is there to help us towards personal freedom and wholeness? But how does this work?

The APS works automatically and appropriately to situations we face in life. That is why it is there. An example might help here. What if you are visiting your local zoo, when suddenly you see a lion has escaped, just ahead. And he is looking right at you. Now, there may be some measured response that would be wise, but immediately, all kinds of reactions kick in within you. Not least of which is the urge to turn and run. You are immediately afraid, automatically. You don't have to decide to turn on the fear. And then, you begin to experience all kinds of physical reactions, all of which are equally automatic. My physician friends tell me that adrenaline starts to flow, bodily functions not necessary for running are shut down, all available blood is sent to the muscles, and breathing gets faster so that oxygen supply increases. And then you run.

Now, can you see that the fear is a reaction to what is being experienced? It is an automatic response to what the eyes have detected: "I see a lion." It is a visual experience that triggers those physical reactions. Now, what if instead of it being a real lion ahead, it was a person dressed as a lion, but I don't know that and think it is a real lion? My inner and outward reactions will be exactly the same. We react automatically to what we believe to be true.

What if we can tap this visualization and mental image process on purpose, towards shaping our self-image intentionally? There are lots of fascinating examples out there of people who have used visualization with remarkable effectiveness. Here are a few of them:

R. A. Vandell discovered that mental practice in throwing darts at a target using visualization improved aim similar to actually throwing darts in practice.[xi]

Natan Sharansky, a computer specialist, who spent nine years in prison in the USSR after being accused of spying for the United States, played himself in mental chess, saying, "I might as well use the opportunity to become the world champion." Remarkably, in 1996, Sharansky beat world champion chess player Garry Kasparov.[xii]

Guang Yue, an exercise psychologist from Cleveland Clinic Foundation in Ohio, compared results of those who did physical exercises to the results of those who carried out virtual workouts in their heads. In the physical exercise group, finger abduction strength increased by 53 percent. In the group that did mental contractions, their finger abduction strength increased by 35 percent. However, the greatest gain (40 percent) was not achieved until four weeks after the training had ended.[xiii]

Alan Richardson reported that in 1960, L. V. Clark conducted a study using 144 high school boys learning to shoot a foul shot in basketball. He divided the participants into two equal groups, where the first group practiced the shot physically for a specified number of sessions, while the second group used the same number of sessions but only used "mental practice" (visualization). Performance was measured at the beginning and end of the trial period. The results were remarkable, with the group using only mental practice improving their success rate by 23 percent, only marginally less than those who practiced physically, at 24 percent.[xiv]

All of these examples point to one dramatic conclusion. Visualized experiences in the realm of our imagination have considerable impact on our personal development. Most likely, intentional visualization can be used to reshape our self-image. Seemingly, the APS does not distinguish between *actual* experiences and *visualized* ones. This is profound!

Richardson also reviewed multiple studies conducted by different researchers over a thirty-year period and concluded most studies indicated that mental practice (visualization) procedures are associated with improved performance. Five studies compared mental practice only, physical practice only, and a combination of mental and physical practice. The trend in all five of those studies was that an alternation of physical practice and mental practice produced the greatest improvement in performance. I will be discussing this more later, but it opens the idea that combining subconscious and conscious techniques in our pursuit of greater inner health will likely produce the best results for us.

When it comes to visualization, A. J. Adams offered some great advice. True visualization, she said, involves holding a mental picture as if it were occurring to you right at that moment. She suggested imagining the scene in as much detail as possible, engaging as many of the five senses as you can. For example, "Who are you with? Which emotions are you feeling right now? What are you wearing? Is there a smell in the air? What do you hear? What is your environment?"[xv]

Now, for some practical application. If you would like to experiment with this, there really is nothing to lose. Try setting a target to spend a few minutes every day, or regularly when your schedule permits, developing your use of visualization. It's a great idea to build this on top of the intentional calmness exercises from the previous chapter. Spend a few moments entering that calm state, and then begin to picture yourself behaving in a way you'd like to or achieving something you'd like to achieve.

Perhaps it is in sports: scoring a basket, hitting a home run, making a touchdown or tackle, or scoring a goal in soccer. Or perhaps it is education: writing a great paper, completing a well-worked quiz, or attaining a needed grade. Or perhaps it is career: achieving a promotion, winning an award, or starting a new job. Or maybe it is to do with relationships: being a loving spouse or parent, finding a new significant relationship, or getting engaged or married. Or life-purpose issues: fulfilling destiny, engaging well in your community, or serving in a nonprofit. Anything and everything. Just create a life experience you can visualize in line with your specific objectives. Develop the ability to see clearly in your visualization, forming vivid and detailed images, paying attention to small details, sights, sounds, objects, and so on. Make it real.

The goal is to create a practice experience. Over time, through repeated exercises, the self-image begins to reshape around these experiences. Once that begins to happen, your APS engages these new traits, instead of the old ones.

This can be powerful when it comes to getting over past disappointments, breaking free from the impact of abuse, or experiencing rejection. Perhaps a relationship went wrong, your fiancé broke off your engagement, or your spouse walked out of your marriage. Or as a child, you were hurting a lot in a broken home and experienced things you should never have been subjected to. Perhaps you were treated unfairly at work or misunderstood in some painful way. These are all-too-common occurrences. You can fill in the blank with whatever your story might be.

While we cannot erase those experiences, or immediately have new better ones to reshape our self-image, we can visualize a different future. We can see ourselves as someone who can enjoy a healthy, sustained relationship, be part of a happy home, or flourish in the workplace. This will help us overthrow feelings of hopelessness that leave us feeling like we are just stuck, as victims of our past.

Chapter 6

Fixing the Past

Things happen. Bad things happen sometimes, even to good people. Emotional and inner hurts can cause inner hardness like callouses, similar to how a scar forms at a physical wound. Physicians typically work to clean up physical wounds, to help avoid infection and prevent physical difficulties developing. With emotional-type wounds, it seems that similar attention would ensure that things like bitterness and rejection do not develop. But at the actual time of the hurt, this is often hard to accomplish. The result is that we can carry hurtful things with us, possibly even for the rest of our lives.

There are many approaches to bringing inner healing to these kinds of things, including professional counselling. It is beyond the scope of this book to delve into that, but I do want to briefly mention two approaches related to this. While much of my focus is on self-development and growth, there is no doubt that sometimes bad or painful experiences from the past are the cause of some serious self-image issues.

For sure, practicing calmness and visualization can help reshape the self-image with positive goals and outcomes to help steer future events and experiences. But these techniques can also be used retrospectively, to help us deal with past hurts or bad experiences we may have had.

Here, the visualization is used to recall the bad experience from our conscious memory and then form an image of a different outcome. Perhaps by visualizing a scene where the hurt doesn't occur, where things end more happily, or where inner hurts are progressively being healed. Over time, those visualized experiences may start to replace the actual ones, as far as the APS is concerned. Then, rather than continuing to outwork the impact of the hurtful situation, it instead steers us towards a happier countenance and the ability to move on. Where we have understandable feelings of inner anger or resentment, these may also then begin to subside. (Note: For more serious and debilitating experiences, including things like post-traumatic stress or serious abuse, I recommend engaging professional help. But you can likely apply intentional calmness and visualization in this way to make some worthwhile progress too).

The other area I want to mention here is the very real need for forgiveness. If we hold on to unforgiveness, it seems like no amount of visualization will fix the inner hurt. Forgiveness is a conscious action, whereas the visualization taps the subconscious. Both are helpful, and the goal is their alignment so they can work together.

Forgiveness is a choice. I remember in the past feeling like I couldn't forgive, because I didn't feel like it. What I have found, though, is that it typically works the other way round. The feelings follow a choice to forgive. But why would I choose to forgive? Simply because holding on to unforgiveness is like leaving the wound festering. Even though things might seem to calm down somewhat over time in the conscious, and the hurt reduces, the subconscious is still very much affected. The self-image may be harboring resentment, or shame, or bitterness. Maybe there is a root of inner anger or even inferiority.

Forgiveness makes sense to us when we realize that all those potential inner traits are harmful to us. We would be much better off without them. I remember past hurts where I chose to forgive, but it felt shallow or even fake. Using the techniques of intentional calmness and visualization can help engage your APS to help. Begin to visualize yourself actually forgiving the person who hurt you and then reconciling with the person. Then, the APS can begin to steer you towards a deeper and more effective level of forgiveness.

The sooner we can forgive, the better. Be quick to forgive. Then, moving forwards, it is great if we can develop an inner value to be a forgiving person. When that becomes established, our self-image and APS are already aligned to engage deep-rooted forgiveness, whenever needed.

I remember a situation when we had a break-in at our home. I was newly married and living in South Africa at the time. We returned from a trip to find that someone had broken into the house and stolen a lot of personal items, including my wedding suit. I still remember feeling the resentment. But then it occurred to me to forgive the thief.

More than that, later I made a decision to actually give from my heart the items that had been stolen. In that way, all sense of loss was overthrown, and I was able to switch potential bitterness into an act of generosity.

It's often hardest to forgive ourselves. Self-condemnation, regret, and remorse all fester when we have experiences we blame ourselves for. We all make bad choices from time to time, so we should adopt an attitude of self-forgiveness. Otherwise, those experiences and feelings fuel the APS to create some kind of payback or personal failure. In that scenario, the very choice that originally resulted in the inner hurt and regret is energized to continue and may even repeat itself.

But here is the real power in engaging our APS for our progress. If we can see the wrong choice we made, and the hurt it produced, as a mistake, it can become a form of negative feedback to the APS. The APS then takes this as corrective information, energizing a refocus towards the real goal instead. Failing at something does not need to make us a failure. Imagine young children learning to walk. They might take a few steps and then stumble. That doesn't make them stumblers; rather, it is just part of the process of them learning to walk.

Chapter 7

Conscious Realignment

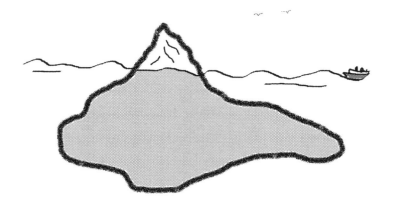

Right from the beginning of this book, I have been trying to present our overall goal as achieving inner harmony. In that condition, all our faculties are working together towards a common goal: things going well. I have focused a lot on the hidden subconscious realm, because that was what I had never been aware of before in my own journey. I had worked a lot on trying to do better in my conscious self over the years, unaware that my subconscious was continuing to work differently.

In addition to forgiveness, I want to outline a couple of other aspects where the conscious realm fits in. First, in understanding how our conscious realm can actually help reorient the self-image. And then second, in how we actively seek alignment between the conscious and subconscious.

Conscious thinking itself can impact and even help control the subconscious. One of the ways this happens is through the area of beliefs. Our inner beliefs are intrinsically connected with our self-image. We have spent some time thinking about how those beliefs are formed through our experiences, but our beliefs are not only formed from experiences we've had. They are also shaped through intentional conscious thought. Engaging our beliefs from our conscious thought and reasoning abilities allows us to impact our subconscious intentionally and, in turn, impact the operation of the APS.

It is a good idea to take time to establish your core inner values or beliefs. Consider writing them down. Then, when things occur that seem to dictate otherwise, you can easily identify those untrue inner thoughts and feelings. You can immediately reassert what you know to be true or what you decided to hold on to as an empowering belief.

Similarly, it is a good idea to periodically reflect on how things are going in your life and examine if you might inadvertently be believing a lie in some way. If that is the case, the APS will be operating accordingly, so you are being driven by a false belief.

An example of a false belief is where we are being hard on ourselves about a past failure and don't believe we deserve another chance. Or where we feel shame that arose from being abused in some way, and we can't see anyone really accepting us or loving us. Or perhaps we had a string of bad grades at school and convinced ourselves we will never be any good at that subject. Whatever the situation, once we unearth the fact that we hold a false belief, we can deal with it. We can reaffirm a positive, hopeful approach and reject the limiting belief.

Another aspect where our conscious faculties can play a big part in helping the APS engage positively is to stay focused on current tasks. The APS works best when it is evaluating feedback and correcting course towards the target. Passivity tends to jam the APS, because it is unable to detect direction. It needs a clear goal to aim at and works best when there is active pursuit of that goal.

Experimenting, or feeling our way towards a solution, allows the APS to receive feedback responses and inputs from those ongoing experiences. It can then operate its corrective action effectively. One exciting result of this is that the APS can inspire sudden ideas or put solutions in our conscious mind that we might never have arrived at through reason or logic alone. When the conscious and subconscious work together in alignment, we experience inner harmony, which is a big part of inner health.

I wonder if we are beginning to get a picture of the kind of lifestyle and habit patterns that will help us make progress towards our life goals and purpose, especially concerning our pursuit of personal inner health, freedom, and wholeness? Our goal is to develop a healthy, realistic self-image of who we are and what we want to be like. We practice developing a state of intentional calmness, freeing up our APS, and allowing our self-image to be reshaped. From that, we develop visualization, putting it to work to help frame experiences that reshape our self-image, as a target the APS can then be engaged with.

In time, this means that our APS steers us to fulfil those things we have now formed in our self-image. All the time, we look to avoid unnecessary knocks and practice forgiveness, including forgiving ourselves. Then we intentionally align our conscious thoughts and choices, developing and reinforcing inner beliefs, while breaking false or limiting ones, and calmly staying active on a forward momentum.

Writing this book is a practical project that is a direct result of me engaging this kind of lifestyle. For years, I held on to a false and limiting inner belief that I would never actually be able to write a book. I made many attempts at putting pen to paper that never worked out. One particular time, I put a lot of effort into researching and developing the ideas I am sharing, only to file it all away for some other day. But I recognized those are false beliefs. Now I visualize myself actually writing a book, finishing it, publishing it, and seeing the joy of watching others read it and being helped by it.

As my own APS began to connect with those corrected inner beliefs, and more specifically that corrected inner self-image, so it began to operate to help me work it out. But I also had to sit down and write. As I did so, I suddenly found myself having increased clarity about how to write this book, what it would look like, how long it should be, what should go on the cover, and even what its title could be. What a contrast. By getting this book published, this is now a reality for me. Thank you for reading it.

Chapter 8

Turning Worry Around

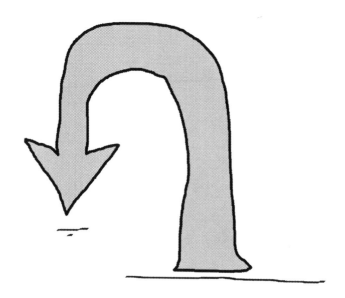

If you know how to worry, you actually know how to engage your APS already. You have been using the techniques we have been discussing. It's just that you didn't realize what you were doing, and you've been focused on the wrong outcomes. Engaging those same processes towards your positive goals will work powerfully in your favor.

What is worry? Worry is imagining unfavorable future results, accompanied by feelings of anxiety, inadequacy, or perhaps humiliation. We experience the same emotions in advance that would be appropriate if we already had the negative thing happen that we are worrying about. We picture the bad thing to ourselves, whatever it is. We visualize it in vivid pictures and in great detail. We even feel the effects of the bad thing happening. We repeat these failure images over and over again to ourselves. This is the worry process at work, and it shapes our inner self-image.

So how about turning that same process into the positive? Instead of thinking negative thoughts about possible bad things happening, rather choose a positive outcome you want and then start to visualize that. First in general terms, and then in increasing detail, forming vivid pictures of what that would look like. Begin to experience the feelings of satisfaction, accomplishment, delight, all out of your visualized success.

To strengthen the visualization, pull up memories of anything that went well in your life, whether related to the current issue or not. It could be as simple as remembering when you first swam a few yards in a pool, passed a quiz, or lifted a certain weight at the gym. Or maybe it was learning to play an instrument, resolve a relationship conflict, or earn a bonus at work. Any success memory will work. Feed it into your current visualization process, remembering what happened in as much detail as possible. This will reinforce those feelings.

Doing this repeatedly over a period of time will shape the self-image, so the APS can begin to engage with it. It's the same as worrying; it's just that the content in this mental imagery is very different.

I just shared that briefly to show you if you can worry, and have worried in the past, you have already engaged the very practices I have been writing about. You can do this.

Chapter 9

When Freedom Fails Us

I have been sharing my journey towards self-improvement and self-fulfillment, and generally my desire to be a good man, where everything is going well. I've been so thrilled with the progress, with the sense of change and new hope. It is incredibly encouraging to discover new things and realize our lives don't have to stay the way they have been. New insight on how the inner person works brought new expectations of ongoing progress.

With all my different inner faculties increasingly aligned, I am able to outwork more and more of who I really am. Instead of my real self being trapped and inhibited, and my self-image struggling in limiting beliefs and brokenness, I am entering increasingly into freedom. Full freedom seems like a great ultimate goal to have, doesn't it?

So far, I have considered our inner health in terms of making positive progress with things, towards growth and freedom. But have you ever thought about how sometimes success is concerned more with restraining ourselves than expressing ourselves? Sometimes, it is wiser to hold our tongue than speak what we really think. Maybe we have an opportunity to manipulate certain situations for our own benefit in business, but doing so would undermine our integrity. Perhaps there are lust issues that, if not restrained, would lead us into compromised situations. We are not only in pursuit of freedom in the normal sense. We must also learn to activate self-control.

Whether freedom actually benefits us really depends on what it is that is being freed. For example, opening a window to allow a bird to fly out of a room it inadvertently flew into feels like a good, positive freedom outcome. But leaving a field gate open so that the farmer's cows escape doesn't seem like such a good result.

We are naïve if we do not recognize our potential for impurity or corruption. There is that tendency that is very real in all of us, and many of our inner health difficulties have arisen from situations where we didn't control that as well as we might have done.

Jesus spoke about some extreme cases of this when He said, "For out of the heart come evil thoughts, murders, adulteries, fornications, thefts, false witness, slanders. These are the things which defile the man" (Matthew 15:19-20 in the Bible).

Even if none of those characteristics describe us, the point is that things that defile us come from within us. If those extreme examples are capable of emerging, we can be sure there are many more everyday self-expressions that are harmful.

Paul, the early Christian leader, elaborated further, "Now the deeds of the flesh are evident, which are: immorality, impurity, sensuality, idolatry, sorcery, enmities, strife, jealousy, outbursts of anger, disputes, dissensions, factions, envying, drunkenness, carousing, and things like these" (Galatians 5:19–21).

That's a pretty extreme list too, and hopefully you don't see too many of those traits in your own life. But perhaps you recognize yourself in one or two of them? I know I did.

As I pondered this, I began to wonder if there could be aspects of the self-image where our success and progress are more involved with developing a self-control element. If so, that does make our pursuit of inner health much less straightforward. It becomes more complicated, sometimes pursuing freedom, sometimes restraint. I remember feeling quite disheartened by this realization, unsure of how to handle the complexity.

It reminded me of one day when I was on a hike to climb a mountain. It looked like I could see the summit ahead of me as I gained altitude, but then when I got to the top of the next immediate ridge, I found myself looking down at rolling valleys and lines of rocky outcrops between me and where I wanted to get to. The summit was way out of reach. Was that the way it was going to be for my pursuit of inner health? Was there always going to be another valley to cross or another ridge to climb? Was the summit always going to be so out of reach?

Thankfully, I discovered a much better, cleaner scenario

I could embrace. There is an upgrade opportunity that can be engaged, to open a whole new level of freedom for us.

Come across to part 3 with me. There we will discover what I believe to be the ultimate game-changer. You won't want to miss this.

Part 3

The Upgrade: A Brand-New Nature

Right in the first chapter, I outlined some of the main faculties we understand to make up our inner person. I mentioned our connection to the five physical senses, the big three of mind, will, and emotions (sometimes called the soul), and then the deeper layers like heart, the subconscious (with its self-image and APS), the memory, and the conscience. How all these work and function together comes out in what we call "personality." But it appears that there is a further part to who we are inside that we have so far not considered. I'm thinking of our human spirit.

What is our spirit? Sometimes, we use the term to describe an attitude or certain demeanor. Or perhaps to do with a particular motivation, or the enthusiasm that comes from being on a joint pursuit with others, like the idea of team spirit. Perhaps it has to do with culture.

All those interpretations are valid, but they do not match what I want to discuss next. Our spirit is a specific part of who we are. It is an inner reality that carries our core identity. It is maybe a bit more than a faculty, perhaps more to do with our inner substance. We find this mentioned in this quote from the Bible: "may your *spirit* and soul and body be preserved complete, without blame" (1 Thessalonians 5:23, emphasis mine).

This is so insightful. Not only does this make it clear that we have a spirit, soul, and body, but also that there is an expectation of completeness and blamelessness. Another way of saying that is, we might become both whole and pure. This seems quite different from the situation we considered in the last chapter, about needing to successfully restrain an inner impurity or corruption potential. If we are whole and pure, there is nothing that needs to be restrained. In that case, we can simply engage the pursuit of freedom, freely, 100 percent. What I discovered about this thrilled me.

We have an upgrade opportunity.

Considering the importance of our self-image, imagine the potential if we could somehow obtain a brand-new nature, one that is indeed both pure and whole. What if we could move from trying to just fix or reshape our self-image, into simply aligning it with a new, incorruptible personal inner nature?

That quote from the Bible above is a clue to where we can discover this. I have not found this anywhere else; it is the Bible alone that presents this opportunity. I discovered this many years ago and sought to engage its benefit in the conscious realm, but it is only as I have come into understanding of the subconscious that this has been able to flourish into greater fullness in my experience. The results have been dramatically improved. From here, retracing my journey necessarily dives into finding out what the Bible actually says about these things, not from a religious perspective, but from the perspective of developing inner health.

In this section, I want to briefly explain what the Bible has to say about these two specific things:

1. Our origin and its limitations, especially when it comes to our spirit and the problem of impurity and inner corruption
2. How we can get a new spirit that can be the basis of a transformed self-image

You don't need any prior Bible knowledge to follow along

with me on this. I will do my best to explain things simply and keep us from unnecessary religious clutter. I will quote from numerous Bible passages and include footnotes that show you where those are specifically in the Bible, with chapter and verse number.

Note: If you would like to check the Bible more widely yourself but don't yet have a copy, you can access it easily and without charge online. One good platform is at biblegateway.com. You will find many different translations there (the original text was written in Hebrew and Greek). I recommend using the New American Standard version, for accuracy.

If you don't like the Bible, or prefer to avoid religious themes, I totally understand. Maybe you consider yourself an atheist. I was there once. But I am so glad I stumbled across the opportunity I am about to share with you. It comes in love, and I really hope you will give yourself a chance to at least explore this remarkable upgrade opportunity. It will allow all we have learned so far to become so much more powerful and effective.

Chapter 10

Understanding
Inner Brokenness

Ｎone of us chose to be born. We had no say at all in our own very existence. Equally, we had no say in how we are made, what we look like, or what faculties are formed within us. It is not like we can choose a specification for who we are, like selecting options when buying a new car. We are who we are. Now, of course, as I have been exploring with you in this book, there is a lot we can do to help shape who we become, or how we outwork what we have. It is not all left to chance, and it is not all out of our control. But our basic substance, and the various faculties we possess, were embedded in us as we were formed in the womb. We are human.

I will turn to the Bible to discover what it says about our origins as spirit, soul, and body. For simplicity and to keep this as brief as possible, I will just enumerate significant unfolding steps. Rather than clutter this chapter with lengthy quotes, I will use footnotes that identify exactly where these points come from in the Bible, in case you want to check that out.

First, here is the creation account:

1. Creator God decided to create a being called "man," made in his own image. This man included both male and female.[1]
2. Jesus revealed that God's core image is "spirit."[2] So, by being formed in God's image, the man was created as a spirit being also.
3. The man's body was formed like a clay figure from the "dust of the ground."[3]
4. God breathed the man's spirit into the clay body. Then, when the body and spirit joined, he became a living being, or "soul."[4] Presumably inner faculties were embedded there at that time. God was then able to form a woman from within the man He had

---

[1] Genesis 1:27.
[2] John 4:24.
[3] Genesis 2:7.
[4] Genesis 2:7.

made.[5] They were then given the instruction to procreate.[6] So you, me, and every other person arrived on the earth through the sexual union of our parents, down through the generations. We are all basically the same: spirit, soul, and body.

Next, we discover the beginning of human corruption:

5. Before Adam and his wife Eve had produced a child, they had an encounter with a fallen angel called Satan, who tempted them to disobey an instruction God had given them.[7] This had a deep impact on them:

6. They knew straight away that they were naked[8] and began feeling the awkwardness of the corruption they had embraced.[9]

7. They had fallen into a state called "death," just as God had warned them.[10] This also marked the arrival of "sin," which then passed down through procreation into all people.

"Therefore, just as through one man sin entered into the world, and death through sin, and so death spread to all men."[11]

8. Understanding the meaning of the words "death" and "sin" is enlightening. The word *death* doesn't mean ceasing to exist, but rather separation from true life. We see the effect of this in a later bible passage that says, "You were dead in your trespasses and sins."[12] *Trespasses* there literally means "fallen from

---

[5] Genesis 2:21–22.

[6] Genesis 1:28.

[7] Genesis 3:1–6, Revelation 20:2.

[8] Genesis 3:7.

[9] Genesis 3:8–10.

[10] Genesis 2:16–17.

[11] Romans 5:12.

[12] Ephesians 2:1.

truth,"[13] and *sin* means, among other things, "to be without a share in."[14] Adam and Eve had "fallen" into a state where they were separated from God, no longer having a share in Him, or having access to His life. They became isolated and in darkness.[15] As the verse above says, that is the state of "death" that has spread to all people, from birth.

9. Our inheritance of this state of death is made clear when we consider the very first parents, Adam and Eve. They only had children after they experienced this Fall and entered the state of sin and death themselves.[16] So although they were originally created in God's image, their children were formed in *their image*—this fallen and "dead" condition.

"In the day when God created man, *He made him in the likeness of God*. He created them male and female, and He blessed them and named them Man in the day when they were created. Adam ... became the father of *a son in his own likeness, according to his image*, and named him Seth"[17] (emphasis mine).

10. Between Adam's other two sons, jealousy set in, and Cain killed Abel.[18] There you have it, jealousy and murder. Sadly, extreme corruption had arrived.

We all have this origin. We were all born into this world with an inner nature that was already corrupted. Our spirit is like God in substance, but not like Him in nature. It no longer has access to His life source, either. Cut off, without

---

[13] Strong's Dictionary G3900, https://www.blueletterbible.org/.

[14] Strong's Dictionary G266, https://www.blueletterbible.org/.

[15] Ephesians 4:17–18.

[16] The Fall happened in Genesis 3. The first account of Eve becoming pregnant is in Genesis 4.

[17] Genesis 5:1–3.

[18] Genesis 4:3–8.

a share, it is isolated and incapable of becoming pure again. It is in darkness.[19]

This was a very brief Bible account of our origin, including where we came from and what we are like:

- In substance we are a spirit being,
- but we have been separated from our life-source,
- allowing corruption potential to manifest within us.

This is a good explanation of why the world is in such a troubled state, and why a new nature is needed.

---

[19] Ephesians 4:17–18.

Chapter 11

The New Creation Solution

W hat an exciting chapter this is for me to write. My memory of when this became real to me is still as vivid as the day itself. It was a cool March Saturday in 1986, in a small suburb of London, England. A neighbor had invited me to a neighborhood rock concert, which she said was being organized by Christians. Well, I drew a blank on that one. What is a Christian? I had grown up in what was becoming post-Christian England and had no personal faith. I was indifferent really; it just seemed an irrelevant topic. But I did enjoy rock concerts, at least the high-quality ones.

The concert was sophisticated enough to have a support artist opening the show, so that was a good sign. The support was a solo act, a guy called Graham, playing guitar and singing. His songs were his own composition, and he enjoyed introducing each one with a brief story about his own spiritual journey at the time of writing it. It seemed like Graham had hit some really low points, including being addicted to hard drugs for a time. But he seemed clean from that now and actually played and sung well. Good for him. I was enjoying it. In fact, I remember thinking he was good enough to make a decent living at this. Why was he hanging out with this religious crowd in a little London suburb?

One recurring theme kept coming up as Graham talked his way through his gig. "Jesus really loves you," he said. He said it over and over. To me, it seemed an odd thing to say. Granted, I didn't know much about religion, but I was pretty sure Jesus had lived a long time ago and had been dead many years by now (like, nearly two thousand years). As I pondered what he was saying, I found comfort in concluding that Graham's mind must have been somehow frazzled by the drugs. He had lost it. But something strange started to happen to me, on the inside. This was completely unfamiliar to me. When Graham finished his last song, I was stunned to realize I knew two things: First, Jesus is actually alive. And second, Jesus loves me.

How did I know that? I have my answer now; this was God making Himself known to me in a personal and loving way, but back then, I was mystified. All I knew was that

I just knew. Jesus loves me. At the end of the event, the organizers were handing out some booklets, including a book from the Bible called "John." I remember rushing home, determined to read and find out more. Just a few hours later, I prayed properly for the first time in my life and asked Jesus to come in and make me new inside. He did. There was no doubt about that, and my life was markedly changed from that day. Ever since, I have been trying to do my best to live out what He had put in me. That's my story.

Now let me explain a little more about how this works, the main points I have since learned and understood from the Bible.

1. The Creator made a way for us all, whereby we can get a new spirit, by being reborn spiritually.[20] That is what happened to me the night of that concert. And when that happens for someone, it does three big things (among many others):
   a. It makes us brand new in the essence of who we are (spirit).[21]
   b. It joins us back to the Creator,[22] so we are no longer in the state of "not having a share." There is no sin in the new spirit.[23]
   c. It opens access to God's own nature,[24] which gives us the potential and ability to overcome corruption.[25] We just need to learn how to do that.
2. Receiving a new spirit happens in a new supernatural and creative act that the Creator has to perform for us, at our invitation. It is a work He does inside us.

---

[20] John 1:12–13, Romans 10:11–13.

[21] 2 Corinthians 5:17.

[22] 2 Corinthians 5:18.

[23] 1 Peter 1:23, Ephesians 4:24.

[24] 2 Peter 1:4.

[25] 2 Peter 1:4.

We cannot do this for ourselves or to ourselves.[26] It is His gift to us.[27] When He does it:

    a. He removes our corrupt record[28] (often explained as us receiving forgiveness of sins, although it is much more than that),

    b. He re-forms us into His image,[29]

    c. He welcomes us into a new eternal family[30] and destiny,[31]

    d. He embeds unique characteristics and gifting that allows us to participate in His bigger plan,[32] and

    e. He comes and dwells personally within us.[33]

All this was made possible because Jesus came to open the way. He came to the earth to open up a new human race, formed with the new human spirit.[34] That's why Graham at the concert I attended made such a big thing about how Jesus loves us.

3. Jesus answered the moral debt of the human race that exists in its fallen state:

    a. By having no inner corruption of His own— although He was born as a man like us, He had no human father and His conception was a supernatural one, by The Holy Spirit.[35] This meant that the corrupt nature did not pass down to Him like it does with every other person,[36]

    b. By first living a corruption-free life where He demonstrated the nature of God by His life and

---

[26] John 1:13, Romans 5:6.

[27] Ephesians 2:8.

[28] 2 Corinthians 5:19, Colossians 2:13–14, Hebrews 10:14.

[29] Ephesians 4:24, 1 John 4:17.

[30] Ephesians 2:19, Hebrews 2:11.

[31] Ephesians 2:10.

[32] Romans 12:4–8, Ephesians 4:15–16.

[33] John 14:23.

[34] 1 Corinthians 15:45, 1 Peter 1:3, Ezekiel 11:19.

[35] Matthew 1:18–21, Luke 1:35.

[36] Hebrews 4:15, Luke 1:35.

teaching,[37] and then by offering Himself as an unblemished sacrificial payment through His death on the cross,[38] when He Himself had no sin or corruption to pay for.

4. In God's incredible wisdom and provision, He assigned the benefit of that payment to every fallen, corrupted person,[39] including you and me. God loves us.

5. Jesus died[40] and was buried,[41] but then rose again from the dead[42] and went physically back to heaven.[43] Through this complete victory He overthrew death: every consequence of the fall of the human race,[44] breaking the power of Satan,[45] and opening the door to freedom and wholeness for all.[46] He Himself declared from the cross, "It is finished."[47]

6. Following His heroic sacrifice, Jesus was awarded the place of ultimate authority.[48] By sending out His Spirit (the Holy Spirit), He opened the new race, the new creation,[49] formed complete in the fullness of His victory.[50]

7. Anyone who acknowledges this and receives Jesus personally[51] can receive a brand-new spirit.[52] In this,

[37] Hebrews 1:1–3, John 14:9–10.
[38] 1 John 2:2, John 1:29.
[39] 1 John 2:2, Isaiah 53:6, Romans 5:18.
[40] John 19:30–33.
[41] John 19:40–42.
[42] Luke 24:1–7.
[43] Acts 1:9–11.
[44] Isaiah 53:4–6.
[45] Colossians 2:13–15, John 12:31–33.
[46] Galatians 5:1.
[47] John 19:30.
[48] Ephesians 1:20–22, Matthew 28:18, Acts 2:36.
[49] 2 Corinthians 5:17, Acts 2:32–33, 1 Peter 2:9–10.
[50] Colossians 2:8–10.
[51] John 1:12–13.
[52] Ephesians 4:22–24.

they are reconciled personally together with God,[53] literally born into a real, spiritual family.[54]

8. He comes to dwell within[55] and promises to never leave.[56] Through this, He establishes them in complete and permanent acceptance.[57]

9. This is a new eternal status, where all fear of judgment is gone.[58] Just as Jesus rose from the dead, those who receive Him know that physical death will not be the end for them. The promise of life beyond the grave is unshakeable.[59]

You can probably tell that receiving this new spirit is not a casual add-on to our lives. It is fundamental, and so much richer than we could ever imagine. I will explain more about this in the coming chapters. The Creator's love is transforming, and life takes on a new focus. Remarkably, we begin an actual relationship with Him. The new spirit we receive has a pure, brand-new, and incorruptible nature. What a difference that makes.

Although we can all experience growth in our inner health by working on our self-image without this spiritual birth, it will always have limits arising from the corruption potential in our core being. If you have never received this new spirit, perhaps you would like to receive it now? You don't have to go anywhere special or do anything religious or ceremonial for this to happen. The motivating force behind the Creator offering this opportunity is simply His love. He wants to welcome you, as you are, and where you are. He is watching, and waiting expectantly!

For many people, this moment brings an inexplicable awareness that this is right. I remember that urge to respond, after hearing Graham tell me at that concert that

---

[53] Romans 5:10.

[54] 1 John 3:1.

[55] John 14:23, 2 Corinthians 6:16.

[56] Hebrews 13:5, Matthew 28:20.

[57] Ephesians 2:17–19, John 1:12–13, Ephesians 1:6.

[58] 1 John 4:17, John 5:24.

[59] John 11:25, John 6:39–40.

Jesus loves me. None of us understand much about what is happening during those moments, but God definitely does. It is literally a new birth, spiritually,[60] and none of us knew what was really going on at our natural birth either.

More than three decades have passed since I took that step of asking God to perform this spiritual birth within me, and I have never regretted it. If you have a sense already that this is right for you, you can respond and receive your new spirit now. You can receive Him. I have a simple prayer that will help you do that. I remember when I did this: I had no religious background and the very idea of praying was totally foreign to me. Perhaps you can relate? It might seem hard to believe that saying a few words in a simple prayer can achieve anything. But trust me, this is powerful. If you are ready, simply pray (say out loud) these words:

> "Lord God, thank you that you love me. Thank you for inviting me into a new creation and the offer of a brand-new spirit. Please could I receive that now? I know I need it. Jesus, I realize this is possible only because you died, rose from the dead, and now have ultimate authority over all things. Thank you that you really do love me. Please come in and make me new, so I can take my place in your new creation family and flourish into all that you have made available to me. Thank you so much."

If you prayed that, know that God has heard you, and He has already responded. Look for changes to start taking shape within you. Some people feel a tangible sense of newness right away. It might release some emotion. For others, they feel little or nothing, but awareness of it grows more over time, as they move forwards. In the next chapters, I will explain more about how this works, and specifically how your own self-image can now be transformed to match

---

[60] John 3:3–7.

that new spirit you just received. This is huge. The new creation is God's perfect solution for each and every one of us.

Just a comment to you though if you didn't feel ready or able to make that jump into the new creation life just yet. That's okay. I invite you to continue reading the final chapters. If you come to realize that this is something you would like, or need to do, you can come back to this page at any time and follow that simple step above. No problem. He will be waiting, and you will be welcome.

Or, perhaps you have received Jesus before but never realized that your new spirit carries so much potential, or that your subconscious can be aligned to engage more fully all that you have received. The coming chapters will likely be life-changing for you.

Part 4

The Subconscious in the Bible

Did you decide to receive your new spirit? If so, that is totally awesome. Congratulations, and welcome to the family. Receiving this new spirit opens a life-changing opportunity to form a completely new self-image. You no longer need to be defined by your past. And you no longer need to reshape your self-image piece by piece. Rather, you have access to a new, complete, fully pure, incorruptible new nature. As you develop your self-image from that, freedom will flourish.

In this section, I will explain how you can renew your self-image in alignment with your new nature. This is not difficult; you just use the same techniques I already explained in this book. The Bible itself contains these same steps and more. In this section, there are three chapters unveiling the subconscious in the Bible. In the first, I share my own journey of discovering this. In the second, dynamic practical activations I have found. In the third, the joy of experiencing relationship in the Creator's love.

Chapter 12

My Big Discovery

Wouldn't it make complete sense that the Bible contains not just the solution for our self-image struggles, but also the means to engage that solution?

The new spirit is a powerful solution for our inner brokenness. It brings a completely new, wholesome dimension to our pursuit of inner health. What I love about it is that it doesn't matter what your specific area of brokenness might be or where it came from or how long you have struggled with it. The new spirit is literally an override. It is a new creation.

For years, I attempted to activate this in the conscious realm and enjoyed significant benefit from that. The Bible has much to say in that area, and I will include some of the most helpful lessons I gleaned in the next section. But the reality was, I had never tapped the subconscious realm. I didn't know there was such a thing. And so, although I was intentional about embracing new creation life in my conscious faculties, my subconscious was left largely unchanged. I had no awareness of my self-image or the APS that was constantly trying to steer my life to align with it.

Although I had become convinced quite quickly that the subconscious is real and very important, it was a big day on my journey when I discovered it in the Bible too. Not only did this validate what I had been learning, it unlocked even more understanding for me. The Bible has very unique and specific insight and instruction I have not found anywhere else. Many people today view the Bible as outdated, like a religious relic from a bygone era. Others might pursue other faiths or be determined to have no faith; they may be disinterested in or wary of what the Bible has to say. And still others might be close Bible adherents but not be aware that it includes these insights (that's where I was for years). My discovery is that the Bible not only reveals the solution of the new creation but also shows us clearly how to engage it, in both the conscious and the subconscious realms.

In this chapter, I will briefly introduce how I first discovered the subconscious in the Bible. In the following two chapters, I will explain unique insights from the Bible on how the subconscious works. This has the potential to lead us into dramatic, rapid progress in our pursuit of personal freedom, wholeness, and inner health.

Discovering the subconscious in the Bible was a big surprise for me. I had been reading this book for more than three decades, completely unaware that it was there. My search began with me not knowing at all where to start. The Bible is a big, thick book, with history, prophecy, poetry, teaching on life and death, and lots more. But after a brief prayer, I found myself reading a short passage where Jesus was commenting on what He called the greatest commandment. That sounds like quite a big deal, doesn't it? He was quoting it from the law of Moses (God's laws to ancient Israel), saying, "You shall love the Lord your God with all your heart, all your soul, all your mind, and all your strength."[61]

This was a familiar passage to me, and one that many in the Bible-faith community would likely know as fundamental and foundational. I had read it many times before, but this time, something suddenly stood out. The way Jesus related this commandment, He articulated four faculties to use in loving God: heart, soul, mind, and strength. This is interesting, because in its original ancient form, the commandment only contained three faculties: heart, soul, and strength.[62]

In very simple terms, one might understand heart to mean motivation or core values; soul to include mind, will, and emotions; and strength to be the idea of vigor or energy. So what of the fourth faculty Jesus added? In the version related above, it is translated as "mind."

I don't know why I never noticed this before, but suddenly, I was intrigued. Many scholars and commentators suggest that the mind is part of the soul. The Bible itself on occasion also references "thoughts of the heart."[63] With

---

[61] Mark 12:30.

[62] Deuteronomy 6:5; this was likely written more than fourteen hundred years earlier.

[63] Hebrews 4:12.

the greatest commandment already including both soul and heart, why would Jesus add *mind* again as a separate faculty to engage in loving God? Especially when it was not separately mentioned in the original text He was quoting. For emphasis, perhaps? Or was there something else going on here?

I turned to my trusted Bible study resource that contained the words of the Bible in the original Greek language (Strong's Dictionary, via the Blue Letter Bible online). To my astonishment, I saw that although the translators had chosen to translate the extra word Jesus used simply as *mind*, it was in fact a different word from the word generally translated as mind, elsewhere in the Bible. The word Jesus used here, in Greek, is "*dianoia.*"[64]

Dianoia does contain some of the same root as the word more typically translated "mind," but it has a prefix added to it (*dia*), which changes its meaning. Now, I am not a linguist or a theologian, but what came out in my further research of this word and its prefix was that it could be translated as "deep thought." Thayer's Lexicon states that the prefix *dia* is "denoting a division into two or more parts."[65] As I found that, I had the sense straight away that this could well be the subconscious. There is a very real sense that the subconscious is both deep, and second part, so that literal explanation fitted perfectly.

Dianoia is not the mind in the usual sense, as in the thought life, where we think consciously or apply normal mental thought or reasoning processes. Rather, this is deeper than that, like a second part. It sounds like the subconscious, doesn't it? What if Jesus was identifying this as a key part of loving God, along with the other three inner faculties He mentioned? It would make absolute sense, because the overall idea here is that we love God with everything we have and everything we are. If the subconscious really exists, it must be part of that.

This same original word, dianoia, appeared several

64 Strong's Dictionary, G1271, https://www.blueletterbible.org/.
65 Strong's Dictionary, G1271, 1223, https://www.blueletterbible.org/.

more times in the New Testament. I decided to test using this subconsciousness interpretation of the word in those passages too, to see if it worked. I also wondered if I might find any sign of a self-image idea or even an auto-pilot system. What about the intentional calmness and visualization techniques we've been discussing? It goes without saying that this became a bit of a passion for me. Was I on to something major that could significantly impact my life and possibly the life of many others? Maybe even *your* life? Had I been missing a huge treasure all these years?

The insights from those dianoia passages were life-changing for me, and I came to one definite conclusion: The subconscious, in the way I had been exploring it, is totally biblical. Not only did my discoveries validate what I had been exploring, the Bible had insight and revelation that went much further, especially in the context of the new creation, our new spirit, and its new inner nature.

Of course, if this was spelled out plainly on the surface, I would have seen it long ago. Rather, in the same way that the subconscious itself is under the surface, we have to look beyond the immediate to see it explained in the Bible too. But it is there. Most of the foundation is in two significant passages, where the word *dianoia* is used. In the first, written by Paul, we discover the idea of our self-image and visualization. In the second, written by Peter, we can find the auto-pilot system and intentional calmness.

Both these passages have some great insights that are more concerned with activation too. I will cover those in the next chapter. For now, here is the basic explanation of the existence of the subconscious in those two passages. Remember, both of these are examining passages featuring the Greek word dianoia.

First, Paul's passage, Ephesians 1:18–19:

"I pray that the eyes of your *heart* may be enlightened, so that you will know what is the hope of His calling, what are the riches of the glory of His inheritance in the saints, and what is the surpassing greatness of His power toward us who believe" (emphasis mine).

The italicized word translated as heart is our word, *dianoia*. In this passage, we see clearly that there are eyes in our dianoia. The word used for *eye* there is the normal word for eye and is taken from the word that means "to see." Strong's Dictionary explains its meaning as including, "allow one's self to be seen, or appear," and also that this has to do with "vision."[66] Isn't that awesome?

Images are things that are seen. Specifically, the self-image is a major part of our subconscious; it's a visual concept, allowing one's self to be seen within. This passage is clearly about an inner or subconscious seeing, because it is referencing the eyes of the dianoia, not the physical eyes. When Paul prays that our inner eyes are enlightened, he goes on to say that the result will be that we know various realities. Do you know what that word "know" means? It means "perceived with the eyes."[67] Again, this is referring to subconscious eyes, not our physical eyes.

With all these clear and specific references, I am very comfortable that this passage reveals an inner image in the subconscious, our self-image. The passage certainly validates my discovery that *dianoia* means subconscious.

The idea that this inner seeing faculty can be enlightened also suggests that we can actively engage this. Not only is this passage introducing the subconscious self-image as a reality; it is also advocating visualization. Visualization is where we actively and consciously develop mental pictures, for the purpose of influencing the self-image inside. What Paul goes on to say is very specific. Here is instruction on what we need to focus on, or visualize, in order to actually reshape our self-image into alignment with our new spirit. We will look at those specific focus areas in the next chapter.

Second, Peter's passage, 1 Peter 1:13:

"Prepare your *minds* for action, keep sober in spirit, fix your hope completely on the grace to be brought to you at the revelation of Jesus Christ" (emphasis mine).

The italicized word translated as "minds" is our word,

[66] Strong's Dictionary, G3700, https://www.blueletterbible.org/.
[67] Strong's Dictionary, G6063, G1492, https://www.blueletterbible.org/.

dianoia. Once again, my purpose is to test this passage, to see if it further validates my discovery that dianoia is indeed the subconscious. Peter is writing that we should prepare our dianoia for action. Immediately that has the sense of activity, behavior, or outworking. It made me think about the auto-pilot system we have been discussing. That is the action part of our subconscious. But the literal meaning of the original words introduces a fascinating further confirmation of this.

The words "prepare for action" are translated from an old metaphor in the original text, which literally means "gird up your loins." This phrase is derived from the practice of the Orientals, who in order to be unimpeded in their movements were accustomed, when starting a journey or engaging in any work, to bind their long flowing garments closely around their bodies and fasten them with a leather belt.[68]

The loins are the place where the Hebrews thought the generative power (semen) resided.[69] Of course, in this case, we are referencing dianoia, not the physical. So this suggests there is a form of inner reproduction in the dianoia. If dianoia is indeed the subconscious, what is this saying? It's saying there is a form of inner reproduction actually in the subconscious. The very idea of the APS in the subconscious is exactly that. It works to reproduce what the self-image contains, after its kind. I'm pretty comfortable that this reveals the APS in the subconscious. Can you see that? And therefore this passage further validates that dianoia is indeed the subconscious.

The final insight to share here is that this passage also advocates the idea of intentional calmness. The phrase is, "keep sober in spirit." The word *sober* means "to be calm and collected."[70] So here we have the Bible advocating intentional calmness, right in the context of our subconscious.

Having set out with nothing but uncertainty, I discovered

---

68 Strong's Dictionary, G328, https://www.blueletterbible.org/.

69 Re: KJV, Strong's Dictionary, G3751, https://www.blueletterbible.org/.

70 Strong's Dictionary, G3525, https://www.blueletterbible.org/.

a very strong validation of the subconscious realm in the Bible, in exactly the way we have been considering it throughout this book. This is where psychology and spirituality find union in the Bible text. Starting with Jesus and the greatest commandment, and then the writings of both Paul and Peter, the Bible reveals the subconscious as a deep mind, or second-part mind, that includes a self-image and an auto-pilot system. It also advocates both visualization and intentional calmness.

In the next chapter, I will dig a bit further into these two passages and explain how they also give unique insight on how to actively engage the subconscious with the new creation spirit, unlocking the pathway into true wholeness.

Chapter 13

Practical Activations

I t is important that we know what we have received in the new spirit. This is the basis of transforming our self-image. But knowledge or theology alone doesn't help us much if we do not know how to live this out. In the last chapter, we saw how two Bible passages reveal the reality of the subconscious realm. But they also give us unique, actionable steps to allow us to engage this practically in our lives. That is the theme of this chapter.

Let us turn once again to the first passage, Ephesians 1:18–19. In fact, I will include verse 19 in full now, and also add verse 20:

"I pray that the eyes of your *heart* may be enlightened, so that you will know what is the hope of His calling, what are the riches of the glory of His inheritance in the saints, and what is the surpassing greatness of His power toward us who believe. These are in accordance with the working of the strength of His might which He brought about in Christ, when He raised Him from the dead and seated Him at His right hand in the heavenly places." (emphasis mine).

As we saw in the last chapter, the italicized word translated as "heart" is our word, *dianoia*. Understanding this now to be our subconscious, which includes both our self-image and our APS, we can understand the first phrase as meaning, "I pray that the eyes of your subconscious [your self-image and your APS] may be enlightened ..."

In the last chapter, we concluded that this is talking about the subconscious eyes of our inner self-image. It is where we are subconsciously seeing who we are. Paul's desire here in his prayer is that his readers would experience enlightenment in that place. How does this happen? Exactly as we have seen earlier in the book: by accessing those subconscious eyes through visualization. It is by visualizing that we are able to intentionally form inner pictures that the self-image can be shaped by. In other words, we can replace what it is currently seeing about our self with something new.

Paul becomes very specific here. He actually tells us exactly what to visualize. He says that the enlightenment is for us to know (literally "see") three specific realities included in the new creation:

- the hope of His calling
- the riches of the glory of His inheritance in us
- the surpassing greatness of His power toward us

(Where it mentions "saints," it is referring to everyone who has entered the new creation. If you received your new spirit, you are included in that term.)

Having our inner eyes opened to these three things will massively change our self-image. It is irrelevant what our past has been. We can reshape our self-image in alignment with who we are now in the substance of our new spirit. And when it is reshaped, our APS will engage with that new target and steer our lives towards fulfilment. It will steer us into a flourishing new creation experience. Without this process, we might be actively trying to engage the new creation life with our conscious faculties, but our subconscious APS would not be in agreement. This would cause inner disharmony and constantly hinder our pursuit of progress from within us. That was definitely my experience for years.

Now for some application. I wrote in earlier chapters how visualization works (see chapter 5). Remember first to use intentional calmness (chapter 4), and then begin to visualize those three things. They are all present realities, because they are all to do with the new creation spirit that we have already received. That is why this is so incredibly powerful. No longer are we focusing on individual areas of our lives, trying to form a new inner image piece-by-piece over time. The inner reality is already fully in place within us in our spirit; we just need to align our self-image with it. We do this by seeing it or by visualizing it.

Let me explain those three things briefly:

- "Hope" means "expectation of good."[71] The "hope of His calling" means God has a calling for us, and that calling is good.

---

[71] Strong's Dictionary, G1680, https://www.blueletterbible.org/.

- We also have an inheritance, which has glory and great riches. In the new creation, we are back in as "shareholders" with God and have become joint heirs with Jesus,[72] possessing all things.[73]
- God's power is towards us, having surpassing greatness. The same power, Paul says, that God used to raise Jesus from the dead and exalt Him to the highest place of authority. Wow.

This is new creation reality. We have all of this embedded within our new spirit, but Paul is praying that we see it. Visualize it. If we don't, even though it is all true in our spirit, our self-image will remain stuck in old, broken imagery and identity.

I encourage you to practice this right now, if you can, or commit to a time soon when you are able to do this. Take about five or ten minutes. First, enter intentional calmness. Then peacefully visualize yourself engaging those three points:

- See yourself secure in God's love, included in His purpose, outworking His calling.
- See yourself alongside Jesus as a joint heir, enjoying all the riches of His glory, having access to and possessing all things.
- See yourself accessing His surpassingly great power. See Jesus rising from the dead in victory, ascending into heaven to great cheers and the applause of millions of angels, and then see that same power being activated inside you.

Remember, as you spend time visualizing these truths, try to focus on details so your feelings become involved. Then the self-image will be impacted, and your APS will become retargeted.

Can you see how powerful this is? Especially if your life

---

[72] Romans 8:17.
[73] 2 Corinthians 6:10, Romans 8:32.

and self-image is contrary to those specific truths, where instead you currently feel rejected, unloved, isolated, excluded, struggling to find purpose, stuck in inferiority or inner poverty, plagued by feelings of unworthiness, fearful of judgment or falling short, powerless, defeated, or trapped in unpleasant or unclean habit patterns.

Oftentimes, if we have been stuck in those kinds of mental or emotional states, it can seem beyond our reach to break out. But now we can. We can engage with the truth of who we are now in our new spirit and visualize the solution. Our self-image can rapidly be changed.

Let us turn now to our second passage: "Prepare your *minds* for action, keep sober in spirit, fix your hope completely on the grace to be brought to you at the revelation of Jesus Christ" (1 Peter 1:13, emphasis mine).

I think it is good to set the context for this passage and its intended conclusion. The next three verses say, "As obedient children, do not be conformed to the former lusts which were yours in your ignorance, but like the Holy One who called you, be holy yourselves also in all your behavior; because it is written, 'You shall be holy, for I am holy.'"

This passage is about lifestyle change. Peter is giving us keys about how to no longer conform to who we have been. Instead, he says we are to be like God Himself. That can sound a bit arrogant to people who do not realize they've been recreated in God's own image already. We have been recreated in His image in our new spirit. What Peter is saying is, live that out now. He references this as being like obedient children. Indeed, we are children, because in the new creation, we become children of God.[74] This is a pretty dramatic passage, going way beyond what our minds might think reasonable. He says this is to apply to all our behavior. The final phrase could be taken as a command to be holy. But I think it also is an assurance that if we activate this new life, we shall be holy. *Holy* simply means "pure."

Notice also that Peter's exhortation is to no longer conform to former ways. For true freedom and inner health,

---

[74] Galatians 3:26 and 28.

we need to bring our conscious and subconscious faculties in line with this. This has to do with our thoughts, our choices, our motives, and also leaving our lusts behind. Lusts can mean anything that drives us to impure behavior or personal overindulgence. Our new spirit doesn't have any of that in it.

Peter wrote in similar vein to Paul, who urged leaving the old and instead living in or putting on the new: "Lay aside the old self, which is being corrupted in accordance with the lusts of deceit, and that you be renewed in the spirit of your mind, and put on the new self, which in the likeness of God has been created in righteousness and holiness of the truth."[75]

Notice the contrast between the old and the new. And notice also the tense Paul uses about the new. This is not something we are trying to achieve, but rather something that we already have. The new, pure, incorruptible spirit in the likeness of God is who we are in the new creation.

So let us look now at our original passage from Peter: "Prepare your *minds* for action, keep sober in spirit, fix your hope completely on the grace to be brought to you at the revelation of Jesus Christ" (emphasis mine).

Remember, the italicized word is dianoia: our subconscious, with the self-image and APS. In the last chapter, we saw how the phrase "prepare your minds for action" is an interpretation of the metaphor, gird up your loins. We saw how this is a picture of our APS, which is steering us towards reproducing what is in our self-image, leading to definite lifestyle change.

Peter tells us to gird up the loins of our subconscious (our APS) by engaging intentional calmness (keep sober). Then he says we should fix our hope. This is our expectation of good. Fix it completely, he says, or more literally just hope completely, unwaveringly.

Wow, that is so strong. No half-heartedness. No mixture. No double-vision. The APS gets stuck if there is confusion. It only works well with a clear target. So Peter says just fix

---

[75] Ephesians 4:22–24.

your expectation 100 percent on one thing: on the grace to be brought to you. Grace is literally spiritual energy that flows out of the favor of God, a word that comes from a root word meaning "joy."[76] Peter says this is brought to us at the revelation of Jesus Christ. In other words, when we grasp Who Jesus is to us and within us, when His nature and life manifest within us.[77] As we already saw, this is all so we then leave past things behind and pursue holiness, the purity that we already have in our new spirit.

How do we apply all this? Let me suggest these steps, by way of summary:

- Take time in intentional calmness. This is essential to disconnect our APS so our self-image can be reshaped. This is effectively girding up our subconscious loins (APS).
- Adopt a position of hope, and hold to it. Decide to let go of thoughts of disappointment and regret, or worrying about future things. Hope is confident expectation of good.
- Begin to visualize the arrival of grace, "that which affords joy, pleasure, delight, sweetness, charm, loveliness: grace of speech."[78] Let go of feelings of not being liked or not qualifying, because grace is God's favor. He looks at you with complete favor because of what Jesus did, not what you do.
- Visualize the grace as coming from the manifestation of Jesus inside you. He is there in your spirit. See who He is, and see yourself as being the same: a picture of purity and wholeness.

The big key in all this is that we are not in the process of trying to become something. Rather it is learning to outwork who we already are. Our new spirit is already fully pure. It was God's creative act within us. These exercises are about

---

[76] Strong's Dictionary, G5485, https://www.blueletterbible.org/.
[77] Strong's Dictionary, G602, https://www.blueletterbible.org/.
[78] Strong's Dictionary, G5485, https://www.blueletterbible.org/.

alignment, agreement, engagement, and, specifically, how to get our subconscious synchronized. Our self-image can be transformed.

There are several more Bible passages written around the word *dianoia*, and each of them has powerful insights on how we can engage our subconscious with the power and potential of the new spirit. I will walk us through those in the next chapter.

Chapter 14

Relationship Treasures

B y engaging our new creation spirit, we are able to reshape our self-image, as we have been learning. But there is another dimension to this that is very important. This is not just a mechanical or robotic exercise. It is also intended for us to develop a deep personal relationship with God. This was never possible before we received the new spirit, because our old spirit was in darkness and separated from the life of God. Paul makes this clear in another dianoia passage: "Walk no longer just as the Gentiles also walk, in the futility of their mind, being darkened in their *understanding*, excluded from the life of God because of the ignorance that is in them, because of the hardness of their heart"[79] (emphasis mine).

The italicized word "understanding" is *dianoia,* our subconscious with its self-image, and APS. Perhaps one reason why I had not previously noticed the reality of the subconscious in the bible is the inconsistency in the translation of this word. This is the third passage we have looked at, but the same word, dianoia, has been translated in three different ways: "heart" (Ephesians 1:18), "mind" (1 Peter 1:13), and now "understanding" (Ephesians 4:18).

In this verse, Paul is telling us to not walk as the Gentiles do. Gentiles in this context are those who have yet to enter the new creation. They do not have the new spirit. They are still fallen and separated from the life of God. Notice the specific phrase that their subconscious is "darkened."

When we entered the new creation and received the new spirit, God changed that, at least in the sense that we have been reconnected with Him now. God is light.[80] We have been learning how to make our subconscious enlightened, or filled with light. All of this is available; we just need to engage it, especially in the subconscious.

In another passage, the apostle John explains that this is so we can know God personally. This was His intention all along. John also references dianoia in this verse: "The Son

---

[79] Ephesians 4:17–18.
[80] 1 John 1:5.

of God has come, and has given us *understanding*, so that we may know Him who is true."[81]

The word "understanding" there is *dianoia*. So our subconscious is there to help us to know God Himself. Isn't that amazing? Our subconscious is such a vital part of who we are. When it comes to knowing Him, the word *know* means "to come to know" as well as "become known."[82]

John goes on to explain more: "And we are in Him who is true, in His Son Jesus Christ. This is the true God and eternal life."[83]

Eternal life is to literally know God.[84]

This book is way too short, and far too brief, to get very far with this. I hope it ignites a desire in you to know Him (or know Him more). I also hope it connects you with His desire to know you. Life lived in that reality is completely different. In many ways, this is the secret to finding true inner health. Becoming one with Him isn't corrupt because He is pure. It isn't dark because He is light. It isn't broken because He is whole.

A relationship with God is a relationship of love because He is love.[85] Our life of wholeness is characterized by living in His love and loving Him back. As we saw earlier, that was the "greatest commandment" Jesus quoted, where He also added in the new word, *dianoia*. "Commandment" to love sounds a bit heavy, and may seem perplexing. It is a commandment, but perhaps it is more an *invitation*. It seems also that this relationship of love is the key to us outworking everything we have been learning. Reshaping our self-image happens best, and easiest, in the place of God's love. And Jesus announced also that if we love Him, we will keep His commandments.[86] Love is the key that unlocks obedience from within us. Paul listed three core

---

[81] 1 John 5:20.

[82] Strong's Dictionary, G1097, https://www.blueletterbible.org/.

[83] 1 John 5:20.

[84] John 17:3.

[85] 1 John 4:8.

[86] John 14:21–24.

characteristics of our new creation life as "faith, hope, and love." The greatest, he said, is love.[87]

Isn't it fascinating that John said God has given us dianoia (subconscious), so that we might know Him. Engaging our subconscious is vital for us to truly live in relationship with God. How much was I missing out on, while I was ignorant on this topic? I didn't even know I had a subconscious. We certainly can't love Him fully if we don't include our subconscious. Jesus made that clear in the greatest commandment. But I have come to believe that we cannot fully receive His love fully either, if we don't engage our subconscious.

Prior to receiving our new spirit, we were separated from God. The verse at the beginning of this chapter said we were futile in mind, full of darkness. That is a fact. Our self-image correctly knew that and owned it as such. Can you see how important it is for us to access our subconscious now and allow that self-image to be changed? Through this process, we get to truly know God personally. As we engage in regular times of intentional calmness and then visualize who we are now in our new state, so God's love can be fully released through our being. Without the self-image being changed to align with this, our APS will constantly be rejecting that. We will be kept back in our old state, with hardness of heart and unbelief.

When it comes to taking time for intentional calmness and visualization, do not plan to spend long periods of time on this. Little and often is better to keep momentum in the APS. In Alan Richardson's summary of the studies he reviewed (see chapter 5), he mentioned that mental practice sessions should ideally not exceed five minutes.[xvi]

There is a process involved in this love relationship that I like to call the "love cycle." I don't have room for that now in this chapter. However, I gave it its own corner of the book at the end. You should go and check that out sometime; it is the energy that truly drives the new creation life.

I will turn now to a final Bible passage featuring the

---

[87] 1 Corinthians 13:13.

word *dianoia*. Are you surprised by how much the Bible has had to say about the subconscious? I have learned so much. In some ways, this last one is the most profound of them all. That is because its theme is very much about how God Himself engages us in the subconscious realm. This is a wonderful, practical expression of His relationship with us. Most of the other passages we have looked at are about us accessing Him, as well as the new spirit He has created within us. Of course, that is hugely valuable. The thought here though of God choosing to get directly involved in our subconscious to access us is remarkable to me. It is so personal.

We find this passage in the book of Hebrews, where the writer quotes from a much older passage in the Old Testament, words originally spoken by the prophet Jeremiah (see Jeremiah 31:33-34):

"For this is the covenant that I will make with the house of Israel. After those days, says the Lord: I will put My laws into their *minds*, and I will write them on their hearts. And I will be their God, and they shall be My people. And they shall not teach everyone his fellow citizen, and everyone his brother, saying, 'Know the Lord,' for all will know Me, from the least to the greatest of them. For I will be merciful to their iniquities, and I will remember their sins no more."[88] (emphasis mine).

There is so much in this passage. As before, I have italicized the word *dianoia*, which we have become comfortable interpreting as our subconscious: our self-image and APS. In this case it is translated "mind." The passage is referencing a new covenant that God would make with His people, Israel. This passage when originally written by Jeremiah was from long before Jesus and before the new creation had been released. That is why it is written as a future reality. The new creation plan was first for Israel, with whom God had a long-standing commitment and relationship. When the new creation was released, it

---

[88] Hebrews 8:10–12.

came first to the Jewish people (Jesus was Jewish), but it then proliferated to everyone.[89]

Jeremiah was a prophet, speaking on behalf of God. He said that for those entering this covenant, God would put His laws into their subconscious, as well as write them on their hearts. I will come back to what I think that means. But first, I want to point out His purpose in doing this. His purpose was a seven-fold package:

1. He will be their God.
2. They shall be His people.
3. No longer would people need to be taught to know Who God is.
4. Instead all would know Him.
5. This applies to everyone, from the least to the greatest.
6. God will be merciful to their iniquities.
7. He will no longer remember their sins.

Can you see the relationship purpose in this? He wanted relationship with His very own people. This comes out strongly in the contrast between two words translated "know" in points 3 and 4 above. Point 3 says that no one would any longer need to be taught to "know" Him. That word has more to do with knowing about or finding out.[90] Whereas the word *know* in point 4 means knowing through personal experience. Significantly, it is from a root word that also means "see."[91] It looks very much again like there is something of knowing by seeing going on here, most likely inner seeing in the subconscious once more. None of us have seen God with our physical eyes.

I love how He says this will be available for everyone and, of course, how He is merciful to iniquities and no longer remembers sins. What a powerful revelation. This new covenant is what underwrites the new creation. All of

---

[89] Romans 1:16, Acts 13:46.
[90] Strong's Dictionary, G1097, https://www.blueletterbible.org/.
[91] Strong's Dictionary, G6063, G1492, https://www.blueletterbible.org/.

this is such powerful and wonderful truth to engage with. But what then of the use of the word *dianoia* in this passage? The above seven-fold package is really the purpose. But the statement prior, concerning the subconscious, explains how this actually happens within us. God said He will put His laws into our subconscious. This is remarkable.

How does He do that? And what does it mean?

The best conclusion I have reached on this is His commitment to co-work with us. As we take all the steps we have been discussing in the other passages, adopting intentional calmness, girding up our subconscious loins, visualizing who we are in the new creation, entering into relationship with Him, God Himself co-works with us to put His laws into our subconscious. Most likely, this means He puts His laws into our self-image. And the result? All seven of the points above.

It looks to me like this introduces another unprecedented dynamic. Whenever we practice any of those techniques, working on reshaping our self-image to align with our new spirit, He Himself is involved. I believe the more we acknowledge Him in this process, the more He joins us in the task. This achieves two invaluable things. First, it changes us more: more deeply, more thoroughly, more quickly. Second, it builds our relationship with Him, as we grow in His love.

The passage from 1 Thessalonians that first introduced us to the idea of spirit, soul, and body seems to confirm this. Let me quote that again now, along with the next verse also:

"Now may the God of peace Himself sanctify you entirely; and may your spirit and soul and body be preserved complete, without blame at the coming of our Lord Jesus Christ. Faithful is He who calls you, and He also will bring it to pass."[92]

Can you see the correlation? This passage says God Himself, as the God of peace, will sanctify us (make us pure), entirely or completely. This applies to our spirit, soul, and body. His goal is that we are complete, preserved,

---

[92] I Thessalonians 5:23–24.

without blame. It is God Himself Who calls us to this, and He also brings it to pass. The reference to the coming of Jesus could have two different meanings. First, Jesus will return one day, and that likely brings more complete consummation of what we are considering. But there is another more present day-to-day meaning too. The word used is *parousia*, meaning "fully manifested."[93] Do you know when we are truly whole, complete, and pure? Whenever Jesus is manifested in us. Whenever His presence is allowed to fill us. Whenever His purity flows through us.

The process of becoming complete is the process of outworking what we already have. In our new spirit, we are complete already.[94] Without that, we would just be trying to improve, piece by piece. But in the new creation, we have access to completion already. This is why the steps we have been learning can be so powerful. Holding completeness as our target is profound. I realized that we can use this as our baseline, engaging with God's own purpose within us and setting our self-image with that reality. I like to use a catchy phrase that keeps me on this track: "The goal is whole."

God loves us, wants a relationship with us, and is committed to work with us in our pursuit of wholeness. All it needs from us is our cooperation. Remember, God says He will put His laws in our subconscious. I was intrigued to see that the root meaning of that word, laws, has to do with "parceling out," especially food.[95] The more we pursue wholeness with Him, the more He feeds us and parcels out more wholeness in every aspect of our lives.

Sometimes, I feel like God is tangibly doing something inside me. Sometimes, after a time of intentional calmness or visualization, I find a stillness on the inside. Sometimes, I have sudden clarity about something I've been trying to figure out, or new certainty on a direction I must take to achieve progress. Now, that is exactly what we should expect when our APS is operating healthily too. I really do

---

[93] Strong's Dictionary, G3952, https://www.blueletterbible.org/.
[94] Colossians 2:10.
[95] Strong's Dictionary, G3551, https://www.blueletterbible.org/.

believe God works with our self-image intentionally, helping shape His laws and His ways there. They then become the target that the APS outworks. Also, as we visualize in this place of togetherness with Him, we can receive prophetic vision and insight, images that come directly from the Holy Spirit. He helps us so much.

Well, there we have it. The Bible has had so much to say on the subject of the subconscious. I hope you found plenty to engage with. In my experience, this is so counterintuitive and new at the beginning, that it might be worth rereading chapters 12, 13, and 14 through a few times. If you take the steps to really engage, you will experience the benefit rapidly. Follow through step-by-step, and watch your inner health begin to flourish.

As I said previously, our wholeness will require us to align with this same focus in the conscious realm too, in our day-to-day faculties. Especially our thoughts, our choices, and our words. The next section addresses how to achieve conscious engagement, once again unpacking vital and unique insights direct from the Bible.

Part 5

Conscious Engagements

We have learned so much about the subconscious and how to actively reshape our self-image, bringing it into alignment with the perfect, pure, and incorruptible new spirit we have received: "Put on the new self, which in the likeness of God has been created in righteousness and holiness of the truth."[96]

In chapter 7, I introduced the idea that we can also bring change to our self-image through practical conscious engagement. In this section, I have three chapters that bring powerful insights in that category. Once more, these come directly from the Bible.

I have found that engaging the subconscious and the conscious in one combined approach is essential to ongoing inner health. One without the other leaves us faltering on one side. There is a lot I could write on the conscious side, as I have been actively working on that for many years now. But I have chosen these three specific topics because they work powerfully in tandem with the subconscious insights we've been discovering.

I believe that with all this working together as a dynamic whole, you will be able to significantly enhance your understanding of how the new creation works. This is your pathway to greater inner health.

Let's get going with understanding what the Bible speaks to us about the conscious side.

---

[96] Ephesians 4:24.

Chapter 15

Talking the Walk:
The APS Reset

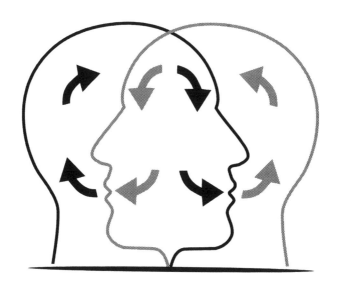

You could be forgiven for thinking we have a typographical error in this chapter title. This phrase is more commonly used the other way round: "Walking the talk." In that context, it would suggest that people might be bold in what they say but are short on living it out themselves. The exhortation would be to live like we talk, practice what we preach. This is all good and sound advice. But turning it around is in response to a huge revelation the Bible announces: Our words shape how we live, so that the way we talk has the power to direct how we walk.

The last three chapters were focused specifically on how the Bible reveals powerful insights into the subconscious realm, by the use of the word *dianoia.* In this chapter, I will look at an equally powerful concept that does not include dianoia, but rather has the *kybernētēs* principle clearly in view. Remember, this word carries the meaning of a "shipmaster" or "helmsman" (pilot)[97] steering their ship into port. This was the word that has been used to describe what we have been calling the auto-pilot system (APS), that part of our subconscious that actively seeks to steer our lives to fulfil what is in our self-image.

Look at how directly applicable this passage is from James: "Look at the ships also, though they are so great and are driven by strong winds, are still directed by a very small rudder wherever the inclination of the pilot desires. So also the tongue is a small part of the body."[98]

Although the helmsman may be the one steering the ship towards port, it is really the rudder that makes that happen. James indicates that our tongue is like the rudder. He is saying that it is our words that steer us in the direction we are heading, which means our words must be strongly linked to our APS, because that is exactly what the APS does also.

This has limitless potential for us. Take a look at what

---

[97] Strong's Dictionary, G2942, https://www.blueletterbible.org/.
[98] James 3:4–5.

James says a little earlier in the same passage: "If anyone does not stumble in what he says, he is a perfect man."[99]

Wow, what an incredible statement.

Make no mistake, our words direct the course of our whole lives. They are directly entwined with the helmsman within us, the APS that seeks to steer our behavior according to what our self-image contains. If the revelation I am seeing here is correct, then this seems to be a way we can directly override the APS to move in a different direction. Redirect it to a new target. Up until now, the idea has been that we cannot do that. Our focus has been on simply adjusting the self-image, because that is what the APS always looks to as its target. It is an auto-pilot system.

Having considered this idea, I have been trying this out. Not just visualizing fulfilment of who I am now in the new creation (although that is powerful and necessary), but also speaking those things also.

I have found that this works on two levels. First, by bringing my words into agreement with what the Bible reveals the new creation to be like. That is essential. But the second level is a complete game-changer. I can use my words to actually speak to my APS.

I have no doubt that the APS exists and is a powerful system within me, but no one ever told me I can speak to it. But I tried this, and it works. You can talk to your APS! You can tell it what new creation reality it is to fulfil, regardless of whether your self-image aligns yet or not. By doing this, the self-image will follow. This is a great enhancement to what we have been exploring so far. Our words are like the helmsman turning the wheel on the bridge of his ship to move the rudder, pulling the entire ship around onto the course he sets. This is classic APS activity. We can literally override and reset the APS with our words.

This is so exciting to me because now I have direct access to the APS and can align it intentionally and quickly with my new spirit, the new person I have already become inside. I can also align the APS with everything my new

---

[99] James 3:2.

spirit contains. The Bible reveals that this is not just a new nature, but also includes embedded specific and unique gifts and calling,[100] through which I contribute to the purposes of God on the earth.[101] Can you see the potential in this?

As a simple and practical example, when I set out to write the manuscript of this book, I had reasons to try to get the first draft written in just a few days. Having never written a book before, that seemed a tall order. But I had learned from the subconscious principles I have shared, and from the Bible, that I have an APS that will work with me to fulfil my inner goals. So I decided to talk out loud to my APS and tell it to adopt the goal to write the draft in five days.

Do you know what happened? I experienced incredible energy and focus, beyond anything I thought possible. And I finished the draft ahead of time. Since then, I've tried this with numerous other inner goals, and the results are remarkable. One thing to remember is that in all APS principles, the instruction given must align with truth. Now, for any specific new creation revelation, that will always work, because it is always true. But beyond that, what I have found is that it will definitely work, so long as we are speaking words discerned to be true, especially the words and will of God for us personally.

Peter introduces the idea that there are specific promises that are the basis of us accessing the divine nature: "Seeing that His divine power has granted to us everything pertaining to life and godliness, through the true knowledge of Him who called us by His own glory and excellence. For by these He has granted to us His precious and magnificent promises, so that by them you may become partakers of the divine nature."[102]

Notice his reference to "precious and magnificent promises," and that by them we may become partakers of the "divine nature." This is so incredibly powerful. Directly access God's own nature. How do we activate that

---

[100] Romans 12:6.

[101] Ephesians 2:10.

[102] 2 Peter 1:3–4.

manifestation of the promises? By our words. By taking a specific new creation promise or truth, and speaking it to our APS. What a joy it was when the penny dropped for me, and I grasped the fact that the APS is the very faculty the Creator put within us, to steer us towards fulfilment of His will and access His divine nature.

Jesus also addressed the power of our words in this way, when He said, "Have faith in God. Truly I say to you, whoever says to this mountain, 'Be taken up and cast into the sea,' and does not doubt in his heart, but believes that what he says is going to happen, it will be granted him."[103]

The Bible narrative similarly reveals that God created the heavens and the earth by speaking words of authority. One well-known example of this is when He simply said, "Let there be light." The very next statement in Genesis chapter 1 is, "and there was light."[104]

You might like to try this. Pick an aspect of the new creation life that you know to be true and then audibly tell your APS to begin fulfilling it, in and through your life.

This is a new concept for many of us, so here is an example to help us understand. Remember, it starts with a promise, so we first need to choose a new creation promise from the Bible that is to do with a particular issue we might be facing.

Let's say I am feeling lonely and disconnected. This was a big issue we discussed when doing our diagnostic checkup on symptoms of the subconscious (chapter 3). How do we set about changing those lonely feelings and experiencing lifestyle change? Well, there are the disciplines of intentional calmness and visualizing, like we discussed before. And exercising forgiveness, where there might be an inner emotional wound. Those are all important. But a big part of how we can make the change is also by our words. Let's find a promise concerning being included and belonging, rather than lonely and disconnected. There are many, but let's just use this one: "So then you are no longer

---

[103] Mark 11:22–23.
[104] Genesis 1:3.

strangers and aliens, but you are fellow citizens with the saints, and are of God's household ... being built together into a dwelling of God in the Spirit."[105]

The key to adopting promises from the Bible is to personalize them. Make them your own. In this example, I could speak these words out loud: "I am no longer a stranger or alien. I am a fellow citizen with the saints, and I am of God's household. We are all being built together into a dwelling of God in the Spirit." (Note: "Saints" in the Bible are simply other new creation people.)

Working with the other techniques we have been learning, I could take a few moments to become calm and then visualize myself in a lively, welcoming, happy community. With all these things in harmony, I can expect my APS to start steering me towards fulfilment. I will find my countenance changing, and the vibe I project towards others will change. I start to become more community-friendly, with a positive demeanor that brings out my true value and worth.

That's just one quick example, but you can apply this to whatever need or symptom you might be facing. Whatever inner belief has been steering you the wrong way, maybe for many years, can change.

One fascinating discovery added to merely speaking these intentional words is that we can also sing them. Something dynamic happens in our connection with our new spirit when we sing songs of freedom: "Be filled with the Spirit, speaking to one another in psalms and hymns and spiritual songs, singing and making melody with your heart to the Lord."[106]

It is a tremendous goal, and experience, to be filled with the Spirit (The Holy Spirit). The implication is that our faculties, and the direction of our lives, are all aligned with Him. Jesus said that the Holy Spirit would flow out from our inner being (our new spirit) like "rivers of living water."[107]

The phrase "speaking to one another" there can equally

---

[105] Ephesians 2:19 and 22.
[106] Ephesians 5:18–19.
[107] John 7:37–39.

be translated as "speaking to yourselves."[108] One way to help us be filled with the Spirit is to speak to ourselves and to one another in psalms, hymns, and spiritual songs. This is a matter of engagement, causing the life from the Spirit in our spirit to flood our whole being. It works well to see this as progressive too, from this verse. Begin with a psalm, a verse from the Bible, move to a pre-penned hymn or song of praise to God with which you are familiar, and then to simply a spiritual song. This could be a simple, personally sung confession of truth and life, engaging with the reality of our new spirit. It can often be spontaneous, made up in the moment. Then, this can climax in "singing and making melody with the heart to the Lord."

Do you see what has happened? The heart is now aligned and engaged also, expressing itself to God. The heart is a motivating faculty for many things, and in this example, it's now being influenced and directed by the Spirit. The heart is the place where faith operates too, so keeping the heart buoyant in this way is tremendously beneficial.

Two last things on the power of our words, briefly. First, a warning, and then a seed thought that I don't have time to develop here, but wanted to just mention.

Here's the warning: An ancient Hebrew proverb states, "Death and life are in the power of the tongue."[109]

So our words work for good and for bad, for life and for death. It is not enough just to spend a moment speaking new creation reality, and then to speak next as if that is not so. Confusion in the APS will cause it to jam, or worse, it will latch on to those negative words and begin steering you towards fulfilling them.

This is pretty challenging for most of us, but I cannot think of a more important discipline to learn than retraining our words. Paul exhorts us, "Let no unwholesome word proceed from your mouth, but only such a word as is good

---

[108] Strong's Dictionary, G1438, https://www.blueletterbible.org/.
[109] Proverbs 18:21.

for edification according to the need of the moment, so that it will give grace to those who hear."[110]

And now the seed thought. Given that the tongue is the rudder, and that our words steer our lives so directly, isn't it interesting what we discover when Jesus first poured out His Spirit to launch the new creation? There was a manifestation of "other tongues" (other languages).[111] This was repeated numerous times after that in the Bible.[112] Tongues is a phenomenon that Paul explained as being where we are able to speak directly from our spirit.[113] He goes so far as to say, even, that our mind is "unfruitful" (we speak in a language we have never learned and do not understand).[114] Almost certainly, utilizing the gift of speaking with other tongues is a direct way we can bring our life direction into alignment with our new spirit and God's purpose. Specifically, Paul says, we can do this without having understood what that means yet in our rational thought processes. This has huge potential for us. You may like to investigate the gift of tongues or explore it further at some point. This is powerful.

---

[110] Ephesians 4:29.

[111] Acts 2:4.

[112] Acts 10:46, Acts 19:6.

[113] 1 Corinthians 14:13–15.

[114] 1 Corinthians 14:14.

Chapter 16

Faith that Works

The new creation offers unparalleled opportunity for our inner health. For many years I had all of its potential available within me, but did not know how to activate it. My life was a compromised mixture of old and new, blended together. In this slightly longer chapter I would like to share the keys I discovered that have changed that for me in the conscious realm. Using these keys in tandem with the subconscious activations I have shared already will allow you to engage a consistent life-flow of new creation vitality. Remember, our inner health flourishes when our conscious and subconscious access the new spirit together in harmony.

The important principle to grasp is that when we receive the new spirit, the old one does not suddenly disappear. That would be great, but sadly that is not how it works. The Bible is clear that we have the old and the new, both existing together. The new is superior but must be actively engaged. Passivity leaves us open to the old fallen nature continuing to dominate us.

Writing to new creation people, Paul says, "For the flesh sets its desire against the Spirit, and the Spirit against the flesh; for these are in opposition to one another."[115] The flesh is rooted in the old spirit, the old nature, separated from the Creator, fallen from truth, given to corruption. In chapter nine, "When freedom fails us," I already quoted what Paul wrote about the "deeds of the flesh": "Now the deeds of the flesh are evident, which are: immorality, impurity, sensuality, idolatry, sorcery, enmities, strife, jealousy, outbursts of anger, disputes, dissensions, factions, envying, drunkenness, carousing, and things like these."[116] Paul's inclusion of the phrase, "and things like these," means the list is not exhaustive: Corruption can manifest in many different ways. But the new spirit is created in purity and completeness. It has no corruption. Whereas the "flesh" is separated from God's life in darkness,[117] our

---

[115] Galatians 5:17.

[116] Galatians 5:19–21.

[117] Ephesians 4:17–19.

new spirit is joined with Him,[118] created in purity,[119] and able to access His own nature.[120] That's quite a contrast. Paul lists characteristics of the spirit life as "love, joy, peace, patience, kindness, goodness, faithfulness, gentleness, self-control."[121] That's a much better list!

Those fruits of the Spirit, as Paul calls them, are a tremendous portfolio of excellent inner health. Having received the new spirit, we have the opportunity to engage all of those traits, and enjoy a life of sustained freedom and wholeness. Each and every one of those traits is constantly available to us. But notice the last characteristic in that list, because it is fundamental in understanding how this works. The new creation gives us *self-control*: the power to take control over our own lives. No longer do we need to remain trapped in past experiences, brokenness, or unhealthy inner impulses. Instead, we can control what traits operate within us and out of us—we can live in the fruits of the Spirit! They overthrow every possible manifestation of inner corruption. This opens to us an exciting opportunity for deep, sustainable, inner health. But how exactly do we do that?

Paul simply says, "Walk by the Spirit and you will not carry out the desire of the flesh."[122] We don't overcome the flesh by focusing on it to fix it, or by fighting it, but by choosing the alternative: our new spirit (which is in union with the Holy Spirit).[123] A simple illustration is to recognize that our spirit is filled with light, whereas the flesh is in darkness. We don't try to remove the darkness, but rather we just engage the light. Here's the good news: Light is always stronger than darkness! And now we have the light available in us. Peter wrote that we have been called out of darkness into God's marvelous light.[124] Paul wrote, "Walk

---

[118] 1 Corinthians 6:17.
[119] Ephesians 4:24.
[120] 2 Peter 1:4.
[121] Galatians 5:22–23.
[122] Galatians 5:16.
[123] 1 Corinthians 6:17.
[124] 1 Peter 2:9.

as children of light."[125] John said, "God is Light, and in Him there is no darkness at all."[126]

Lean in here, because I want to explain step by step how we can actually do this. We can adopt this personally and find it to be the pathway to great freedom, the pathway to thriving inner health. Again, this opens up the possibility for rapid change because everything we need is already in us.[127] We just need to engage. Nothing of the old needs to hold us any longer. We can live in the new creation. I haven't discovered a single Bible passage that explains the power basis in this more clearly than this one written by Paul: "I have been crucified with Christ; and it is no longer I who live, but Christ lives in me; and the life which I now live in the flesh I live by faith in the Son of God, who loved me and gave Himself up for me."[128]

I first began to come into this understanding many years ago, when I was working on staff pastorally at a church in South Africa. I was definitely trying to pursue a life of purity and wholeness, but didn't understand yet how. At this particular time, I was reeling from having spent time visiting with a Christian community that was heavily focused on sins and the need to be holy. Their theory went something like this: You must confess every actual sin you can think of that you are guilty of committing, so you can be forgiven and cleansed. If you do that, you will gradually get more holy. You might even get healed of sickness and disease along the way. The whole community was consumed with their sinfulness. This is not the new creation.

The new creation is all about being consumed with our righteousness, not our sinfulness. Focus on the spirit, not the flesh. Live in light, not darkness. Thankfully, all those years ago, my brother-in-law, Ron Robinson, corrected my focus, when he said to me, "You will never become holy by focusing on the flesh."

---

[125] Ephesians 5:8.

[126] 1 John 1:5.

[127] 2 Peter 1:3–4.

[128] Galatians 2:20.

Here is an interesting anecdote: Ron was the lead pastor at the church I was serving in, and I had gone to tell him I needed to step out of my responsibilities because I was overwhelmed with how sinful I was feeling. That was the fruit of engaging the approach I had encountered at that community. Ron told me straight, to focus on who God had made me in the new creation, and to go and get on with my job.

Let's track through now what Paul is saying in Galatians 2:20. This is the how-to when it comes to us intentionally accessing the new creation life by our active and conscious engagement. For brevity, I will just articulate the four clear steps he introduces and then comment on them.

1. I have been crucified with Christ.

   This is a critical truth to engage, although it might be a hard one to grasp. I do not recommend trying to fully understand this concept from a human logic perspective, but rather through spiritual discernment. Understanding will sink in if you just choose to agree with it and accept it. When Jesus was crucified on the cross to make payment for our fallenness, we were crucified *with Him* spiritually. He Himself said this would happen, saying that when He was lifted up from the earth (on the cross), He would "draw all people to Himself" there.[129] Perhaps the easiest way to grasp this is to accept that, although this happened at a definite moment in time long ago, it was an eternal spiritual act. By God's doing, we were added there with Him, and so His death was also our death. Notice the tense Paul used. This is not something we are trying to achieve. We are not trying to crucify the flesh, but rather we are just agreeing and aligning with something God already did. We are identifying with it personally. Knowing this is true, we can obtain all the benefit. Engaging

---

[129] John 12:32.

the death is the basis of cutting off the power of the flesh. Paul says elsewhere that those who have died are freed from sin.[130]

2. It is no longer I who live but Christ lives in me.

    Paul doesn't mean he doesn't live any more, because he was still writing the letter. He is talking about identity and life source. No longer do I live out of my separated, dark, corrupt, independent self (the flesh), but instead I am living from the life of Jesus Himself, Who is in my spirit. I am joined with Him there, and He is living in me. Our goal is that Jesus is seen through our lives, a bit like He modeled with reference to the Father, when He said, "He who has seen Me, has seen the Father."[131]

3. The life which I now live in the flesh I live by faith.

    "Flesh" in this instance isn't the same as the corrupt nature I have been referencing earlier. Rather, this is a term meaning the natural realm, or the physical body of a person. Both meanings can be taken from the same word, which can be confusing. Paul does not advocate "living in the flesh," as in the corrupt nature. But he was living presently in the physical here and now. He is saying that as he does that, he lives by faith. The life he lives, he lives by faith. This is critical. Engaging the new creation is all by faith. I'll comment more on this below, specifically on how we actually live by faith.

4. In the Son of God who loved me and gave himself up for me.

---

[130] Romans 6:7.
[131] John 14:9.

Faith has to have focus, and Paul's focus was singular: "I live by faith in the Son of God." In other words, faith in all that Jesus is, all that He did, and all that He has released to us in the new spirit, the new creation. But notice two things Paul highlighted. First, that Jesus loved Him. Everything we have in the new creation is fueled by the love of Jesus. We cannot live out this new life from any other start point (see the section on the "love cycle" after the epilogue). And second, that Jesus gave Himself up for Paul (and us). When Jesus hung on the cross, the last thing He said was, "It is finished."[132] He fully paid the price. There is nothing left for us to pay.

I have found that there are two keys that help us actively apply those four steps. These keys open up the freedom of the new creation, drawing ever-flowing life from our pure new spirit. The two keys are *identification* and *faith*. Identification is where we actively take what Jesus did for everyone, and make it our own personally. Faith is where we then choose to live in that reality.

Identification

God is very practical and gave us two simple ways to embrace identification—water baptism and communion. First, let us look at water baptism. Baptism in water is our opportunity to identify with what Jesus did for us, and make it our own personally. Baptize means "immerse" and engages us with Jesus in His journey of victory, from His death right through His burial, resurrection, ascension, and emergence in heaven in glory and ultimate authority.

Water immersion can happen anywhere there is enough water. I have had the privilege of baptizing (immersing) believers in a church baptism tank, a swimming pool, a river, an ocean, even a bath tub! But what is the point of

---

[132] John 19:30.

this? Paul says baptism is our burial with Jesus,[133] which only makes sense if we have agreed that we also died with Him: "I have been crucified with Christ." By being "buried" under the water, we affirm our death with Him, but more than that our will engages with His ongoing journey through burial and on into His emergence from the grave. We are raised with Him into the power of new creation life![134] This is most likely what Jesus meant when He said His disciples must take up *their* cross and follow Him.[135] It is making His cross our cross, His death, our death, and when we do that we follow Him into His burial and rise into the power of His resurrection. That is His purpose. We can then live fully in His ways, which is not possible in our old, fallen state. Once we have been baptized, new creation faith is much easier.

Water baptism is not needed to get us out of judgment and into the new creation, or even into heaven after our physical death, but it is powerful in our pursuit of new creation freedom and wholeness in this life. Jesus said simply it is those who do not believe who remain condemned, but it is those who believe *and are baptized* who shall be saved.[136] Saved is the Greek word "sozo", which means to be made whole.[137] It is translated many different ways in the Bible depending on the issue being addressed. This includes where people are healed,[138] delivered,[139] physically strengthened and restored,[140] rescued from evil,[141] even raised physically from death.[142] The solution of God potentially meets us at every need.

Water baptism carries two dynamic elements powerfully illustrated by ancient bible stories: one pointed out by Paul,

---

[133] Romans 6:4.

[134] Romans 6:5.

[135] Matthew 16:24.

[136] Mark 16:16.

[137] Strong's Dictionary, G4982, https://www.blueletterbible.org/.

[138] Matthew 14:36.

[139] Luke 8:36.

[140] Luke 8:43–48, Acts 4:9 (reference Acts 3:1–8).

[141] 2 Timothy 4:18.

[142] Luke 8:49–50.

and the other by Peter. The one Paul mentions is when the Israelites crossed through the parted waters of the Red Sea, only to see the water crash back in and drown the Egyptian armies that were chasing after them.[143] Their "baptism" in the sea cut off the pursuit by their enemies. By implication, whatever issues, habits, tendencies, or strongholds follow us from our past, the victory of Jesus at the cross has defeated them, and our baptism identifies us with that victory. (Note: Paul continues in that passage with a warning that the Israelites did not enjoy all the benefit of their baptism because they still craved evil things. They did not have the privilege of a new creation back then and were still bound by the impulses of the flesh in unbelief. Paul exhorts us to pursue the freedom we have now in Jesus).[144] The second story is one pointed out by Peter, that illustrates our security, protection, and assurance in our new creation status. This is taken from when Noah and his family were saved in the ark when the huge floods wiped out everything else.[145] Peter says, "Corresponding to that, baptism now saves you." We are saved and safe in Jesus in the new creation, protected from judgment and freed from condemnation.[146]

Paul summarizes the impact of baptism so powerfully in this passage from Colossians:

> "...having been buried with Him in baptism, in which you were also raised up with Him through faith in the working of God, who raised Him from the dead. When you were dead in your transgressions and the uncircumcision of your flesh, He made you alive together with Him, having forgiven us all our transgressions, having canceled out the certificate of debt consisting of decrees

---

[143] Exodus 14:21–30, 1 Corinthians 10:1–2.

[144] 1 Corinthians 10:5–11.

[145] 1 Peter 3:18–22.

[146] Romans 5:9, Romans 8:1, 1 Thessalonians 1:10.

against us, which was hostile to us; and He has taken it out of the way, having nailed it to the cross."[147]

Engaging the faith walk of Galatians 2:20 will be easier when we are baptized, because we have already settled the issue of identification with Jesus. We have taken ownership of all He did for us. If you have been baptized already, simply engage that truth as you proceed. If you have not yet been baptized and would like to be, find a believer in Jesus who is willing to do that for you, or ask at a Bible believing church.

While on the subject of baptism, there is another baptism that Jesus called being "baptized in the Holy Spirit." Baptism in the Holy Spirit immerses us into union with Him, and joins us spiritually in His body with our fellow believers.[148] This is a primary objective in the mission of Jesus, as all four gospels introduce Him as the One who baptizes in the Holy Spirit.[149] For many people, this baptism is a dynamic experience that brings strong new creation manifestations like joy, deep peace, or the sense of God's love, as well as the release of spiritual gifts.

Becoming baptized in the Holy Spirit allows all our inner faculties to fully embrace His freedom. As Paul writes, "Where the Spirit of the Lord is, there is liberty (freedom)."[150] I remember when I first experienced this baptism: I was overwhelmed by God's love, which triggered an upsurge of gratitude and delight from within me. There were no words to express that fully until I suddenly began speaking in an unknown spiritual language. It was like bursting into limitless, extravagant praise![151] I would love to share more on baptism in the Holy Spirit, but that is beyond the scope of this book. You might like to investigate it further, or simply

---

[147] Colossians 2:12–14.
[148] 1 Corinthians 12:12–13.
[149] Matthew 3:11, Mark 1:7–8, Luke 3:16, John 1:33–34.
[150] 2 Corinthians 3:17.
[151] Acts 10:46.

ask Jesus to baptize you in His Spirit, or ask another believer familiar with this to pray with you to receive it.

Having explored the importance and power of identification through water baptism, and noted the supernatural potential in Holy Spirit baptism, let us now briefly consider communion, the second practical way to engage identification. Whereas water baptism is a once-only act, communion is an activation we can use on an ongoing basis. In communion, bread is used as an emblem of the body of Jesus that was crucified, and wine (or other substitute) an emblem of His shed blood. On His body He took the full force of overthrowing the power and consequence of humanity's fallenness, and it was His shed blood that sealed the new covenant that underwrites the new creation solution. Jesus introduced communion at the Last Supper, on the night before He was crucified. As part of the Passover meal, He gave the bread and wine to His disciples to take, but also said they were to take this after, in remembrance of Him.[152]

Paul wrote about communion also, stating specifically that it is a way we can "proclaim the Lord's death."[153] As we take the bread and wine we identify with what Jesus did at the cross, making it our own. Paul said we must examine ourselves to make sure we do this in a worthy manner, meaning that we do it in humility by faith, and by honestly applying it to our lives. There are many testimonies of people who have experienced breakthroughs with physical healing or other types of well-being as they do this. On occasion I have found it helpful to take communion when I need a tangible way to engage my faith with Jesus's victory on my behalf, especially when I begin to experience symptoms of sickness. We can take communion anywhere, either alone or with other believers. Communion is not an empty ritual or religious observance, but a practical engagement with God's power. Approaching it only ceremoniously or half-heartedly is an example of taking communion in an "unworthy manner." Doing that will mean it may have little

---

[152] Luke 22:19–20.
[153] 1 Corinthians 11:23–32.

effect, causing Paul to comment that people may remain sick or even die.[154]

Having considered the first key of identification, using the practical activations of baptism and communion, let us now move on to our second key—faith. How do we walk by faith in the way Paul suggests in those four steps in Galatians 2:20?

Faith

Faith is an active approach to life and does not work in passivity. As we actively choose to live this way and continue to work on our subconscious to ensure alignment there also, we can experience quick, sustainable change. Deep inner health is here.

Faith was a problem for me for years. What do you do if you don't seem to believe something? Or believe it enough? I lamented, "If only I had more faith." Elsewhere, Paul calls faith an act of obedience.[155] Faith isn't something that either mystically exists or doesn't. Faith is more to do with choosing to agree with truth. What I have found is, if I do that, "faith manifests."

If you are struggling with whether you believe or not, just decide that you *do* believe. Then see what happens. The only other option you have, ultimately, is to decide instead that you *do not* believe. Without wanting to be overly blunt, the Bible describes that position as having an evil, unbelieving heart.[156] There is not much growth potential for any of us there.

Paul explained faith in terms of the "word of faith," which in Romans 10 he said is near to us.[157] Specifically, he said faith is "in our heart and in our mouth,"[158] and that, "with

---

[154] 1 Corinthians 11:30.
[155] Romans 1:5 and 16:26.
[156] Hebrews 3:12.
[157] Romans 10:8.
[158] Romans 10:8.

the heart a person believes, resulting in righteousness, and with the mouth he confesses, resulting in salvation."[159]

There are two parts here to the walk of faith. First, the heart part, which is where we actually believe or agree, and then second, the mouth part, which is how we confess or speak. The result? Righteousness and salvation. Righteous means standing right with God, and salvation is from that same "sozo" word we saw earlier, that means "to be whole, or become whole."[160]

Do you see how this ties in with the rudder of the ship and the power of our words? The faith walk starts with the choice to believe. But then we need to speak it. Elsewhere, Paul said, "But having the same spirit of faith...we also believe, therefore we also speak."[161]

Let me give a brief example of how this all works. Imagine for a moment that I am struggling with disliking someone. Perhaps it outworks in anger, or jealousy, or even violent thoughts or acts. What do I do with that? Well, first of all, I don't try to fight it. Rather, I set about intentionally overcoming darkness with light. Of course, as we have seen before, if there is unforgiveness, that will hinder, so forgiveness is an essential beginning. Jesus said, "Whenever you stand praying, forgive."[162] Then, I address the dislike directly. I say out loud, "I am crucified with Christ. I choose no longer to live in my old fallen state of disliking people. Instead, I live out of the life of Jesus within me, and so now I love."

I could then repeat this, inserting the name of the person I dislike. This is so powerful. Alignment with the death of our old corrupt nature (the flesh) breaks its power. Then agreement with who I am in the new, pure, new creation spirit, engages its life. But there is one third part that seals this in the walk of faith. I live this when I then act

---

[159] Romans 10:10.
[160] Strong's Dictionary, G4982, https://www.blueletterbible.org/.
[161] 2 Corinthians 4:13.
[162] Mark 11:25.

accordingly. James says, "Faith without works is dead."[163] So I believe (agree), speak, and then act. In this case, I would choose to act in a loving way towards the person I dislike. Pausing, entering intentional calmness, and visualizing myself doing that will help align my subconscious and set the APS to help me succeed.

That is the lifestyle of walking by faith. We can apply it to any issue we may be facing. The victory of the cross is absolute and its power is available to us, potentially meeting us at the point of every possible need. We can experience wholeness. Adopting a lifestyle of actively living by faith in this way aligns our conscious realm perfectly with all that we have learned about reshaping our self-image, and setting our APS towards freedom and wholeness. With our conscious and subconscious in harmony, we can experience the reality of all that is embedded in the new creation.

Let's look at that list of spiritual fruit again. We can have a life filled with these qualities when we learn to walk by faith like this: the fruit of the spirit is "love, joy, peace, patience, kindness, goodness, faithfulness, gentleness, self-control."[164]

Do you remember the diagnostic checkup we considered in chapter 3, where we were trying to discover the condition of our inner self, or self-image, through symptoms? Now we have a new list of positive symptoms: love, joy, peace, patience, kindness, goodness, faithfulness, gentleness, and self-control. Where these are our experience, we know we are walking well by the spirit, our new inner nature. Where they are not, we know we need to adjust and begin drawing from our spirit.

One last thought around this lifestyle of walking by faith and walking by the spirit: Inner health is about inner harmony, with all our faculties working together as one. In addition to aligning our subconscious in the way I described previously and choosing, speaking, and acting the way I just outlined, we are also able to intentionally control our conscious thought

---

[163] James 2:17.

[164] Galatians 5:22–23.

life. The mind is a big potential battlefield, but we can take control there. It's much easier to do this if we are already walking the faith walk and also aligning our subconscious. In this regard, Paul teaches that we are to literally *set our mind* on the spirit: "For those who are according to the flesh set their minds on the things of the flesh, but those who are according to the Spirit, the things of the Spirit."[165]

He then states this vivid contrast: "The mind set on the flesh is death, but the mind set on the Spirit is life and peace."[166]

The easiest way I found to do this is, again, to simply say out loud, "I set my mind on my spirit." As we discussed, this turns the rudder and steers our conscious mind to engage our spirit nature, rather than our flesh. It is also good at this point to speak to our APS directly as well and tell it to adopt as its target our mind being set on our spirit. In line with this, we can also actively and intentionally decide to think about wholesome things: "Whatever is true, whatever is honorable, whatever is right, whatever is pure, whatever is lovely, whatever is of good repute, if there is any excellence and if anything worthy of praise, dwell on these things."[167]

When I realized that this is all under my control, I suddenly saw that inner health really was in reach. It matters not what we experienced in the past, or what things throw themselves at us in the present; we can walk by faith and live the new creation life.

---

[165] Romans 8:5.
[166] Romans 8:6.
[167] Philippians 4:8.

Chapter 17

Setting Our Course

I n chapter 7, I explained the principle of actively reshaping our self-image by consciously adopting a set of core inner beliefs. When we do that, our APS works within us to guide us by those beliefs. It works as the helmsman to get us to port. In the last two chapters, I explained practical ways to engage our conscious realm to do this. This is always an active engagement, never a passive attitude.

In this chapter, I want to just outline five fundamental characteristics of the new creation that can help frame a solid inner belief framework. It is like setting our course. Before we entered the new creation, we likely had a complex mixture of beliefs, many we probably didn't even know about, but they shaped the direction of our lives. Some came from past experiences, others from things we heard, still others from the culture we are surrounded by. But in the new creation, we have a powerful reset opportunity. We can adopt a clear, whole belief framework to live by. This brings such inner security, confidence, and peace.

What is powerful about using specific new creation truth is that it's not something we are trying to create or make up. It is already true. After we receive the new creation spirit, we have this within us. All we are doing here is trying to articulate what that is, so we can align every part of us with it, including our APS.

For simplicity, I arranged these five fundamental characteristics around the acronym "WHOLE." It might be good to add a visualization exercise where you see yourself on the ship, being steered to port. Visualize the port's name on a big sign next to the harbor wall. The port's name is "Whole." This is the new creation life. Remember that catchy phrase of mine: "The goal is whole."

Here are the five characteristics. These are the crystalized priorities I gradually formed over more than three decades, in pursuit of conscious wholeness. You might like to adopt these also.

- **W**ho Am I?
- **H**ope Unshakeable
- **O**ne Together
- **L**ive It Out
- **E**mpower Others

I will just make very brief statements about each one and include some Bible verse references in the footnotes. Each of these could be a book in itself (note to self)! These fundamental characteristics have helped shape my life, but have been marvelously unleashed since I learned how to align my subconscious around them also. This framework has become one of the keys to my inner health. I feel so secure and confident knowing who I am, where I stand with God, and how this all outworks into new creation vitality.

Who Am I? This has to do with our identity and is absolutely essential for self-image transformation. If we don't know who we are in the new spirit, our self-image will dictate from its own understanding, from our past. And the APS will work to continuously reinforce that. We need to reshape our self-image around who we really are now. There is so much on this, but briefly, I want to mention two things. First, I am a new creation. I am not who I was. Paul tells us that old things have passed away and new things have come.[168] Second, by virtue of spiritual birth, I have become a son of God. He is my Father. I am in His family. I belong, and I have an inheritance. Sonship in this regard is both male and female; there is no distinction spiritually.[169]

Hope Unshakeable. I have mentioned hope quite a lot in this book. It really is a big deal. Archbishop of Canterbury Justin Welby said that biblical hope is "the certain expectation of something not yet seen."[xvii] In simple terms, hope can be taken to mean "expectation of good."[170] We can apply that to

---

[168] 2 Corinthians 5:17.
[169] Galatians 3:26–28.
[170] Strong's Dictionary G1680, https://www.blueletterbible.org/.

literally everything in our lives. There is so much negative, pessimistic thinking in this world: worry, self-doubt, fear. The Bible says we are born again into a living hope.[171] We need to reshape our self-image and our inner beliefs around that truth. And this applies not just in this life. In fact, Paul said, "If only for this life we have hope in Christ, we are of all people most to be pitied."[172] No, we have genuine hope for eternity too. We will make it. Jesus said we have already passed out of judgment into life.[173]

I love this passage by Jude. It's a good one to memorize and hold to in our inner belief framework: "Now to Him who is able to keep you from stumbling, and to make you stand in the presence of His glory blameless with great joy, to the only God our Savior, through Jesus Christ our Lord, be glory, majesty, dominion and authority, before all time and now and forever."[174]

Interestingly, by quoting Jude here, I have now referenced writings by every biblical author in the New Testament: Matthew, Mark, Luke, John, Paul, Peter, James, Jude, and the writer to the Hebrews. My themes and content in this book are intrinsically embedded across all the Bible writers.

One Together. Our relationship with God is much deeper than we could ever have imagined. In our new spirit, we become one with Him.[175] Jesus's prayer before His death was that all who receive His life would become one together.[176] So, this is not just about you and Him, or me and Him. It is about us and Him. I'll have more to say on this in my final chapter. But this sense of togetherness and union creates two specific opportunities for us that are not accessible anywhere else on the planet. The first is, we become part of a dynamic community, where we are all baptized spiritually into one

---

[171] 1 Peter 1:3.

[172] 1 Corinthians 15:19.

[173] John 5:24.

[174] Jude 24–25.

[175] 1 Corinthians 6:17.

[176] John 17:20–23.

body.[177] When this is operating correctly, there is nothing to match it in terms of value, belonging, and welcome. It is the bedrock of hospitality and of living in the love of God. Linked directly to this, secondly, is an overflow into witness, where we are able to represent God to the world. Jesus said we would even do the kind of works He did and more.[178] In that prayer in John 17, Jesus said that when we live in this one-together reality, the world will notice two things: First, that Jesus really did come from heaven to help us. And second, that we are loved by God in the same way that He is.[179] That is enormous. Being loved manifestly by God helps us overcome all the different aspects of inner brokenness and lack of inner health.

Live It Out. Quite simply, this engagement with the new spirit is not just about theory or theology. We are able to experience real lifestyle change. The inner purity we receive can be lived out. Of course, there are steps to achieving that, which include both the conscious and the subconscious. Many of us have had a self-image that is fixed more on "can't do" than "can do." Doubtless, there are reasons for that. Embracing the core new creation truth that I can do this is in itself life-changing. But also, actively engaging wholeness is fueled further by the confidence of what we have been learning. We now know what the subconscious is and how it works. We know how we can reshape our self-image and allow our APS to steer us in the way of life. And we know several ways we can activate this intentionally in the conscious realm too, including by our words, by our walk of faith, and now by creating this framework of core beliefs. We can live it out.

Empower Others. Making this shift might be close to unthinkable for some readers. The reality is that "hurt people hurt people. Broken people break people." When we feel hurt or broken, we can feel like we have nothing to give. But as we

---

[177] 1 Corinthians 12:13.

[178] John 14:12.

[179] John 17:23.

pursue a wholeness from the new spirit within us, so we can move swiftly into better inner health. Out of our relationship with God, we can then begin to become fruitful also, in helping others grow. I think, for all of us, we need an element of this. We were created that way. Now, in the new creation, we have the ultimate ability to do so. It is potentially limitless. Adopting a core belief that we can empower others will help overthrow feelings of worthlessness. We can embrace value and add value to others. There are many ways we can participate, and each of us will likely have our own unique way. I love that. But there is an underlying principle too that applies for all of us. As we experience wholeness, we develop living fruit. In that fruit will be seed that we can sow into others. And by that, we can add value wherever we may be, in whatever role we may have in life. It comes down to us becoming confident in who we are, living it out, and then passing it on. Paul revealed this powerful principle to Timothy, whom he called his son: "You therefore, my son, be strong in the grace that is in Christ Jesus. The things which you have heard from me in the presence of many witnesses, entrust these to faithful men who will be able to teach others also."[180]

Can you see the multiplication power in this? When we pass on what we have, we can pass it on to people who will pass it on to others also. And then they too will do the same. There is no way of knowing how far this might reach, if we will just engage. It is not just how many seeds are in an apple, but more, how many apples are in a seed. Embracing this belief will unleash a tremendous sense of life purpose.

Adopting these five WHOLE characteristics establishes an inner framework for life. You can build on this with specific aspects that apply to you personally. Holding to these core inner beliefs will establish stability in your self-image, causing your APS to guide you resolutely towards the port called Whole.

---

[180] 2 Timothy 2:1–2.

Part 6

Ultimate Purpose

The new creation inner beliefs I shared in the last chapter provide a tremendous framework for a fruitful lifestyle; a life lived in flourishing inner health.

However, there is something more I must share in the book's final part. Although I have touched on this here and there, I want to leave you with a clear vision of what I have come to believe is our ultimate purpose. When I first grasped this, it was completely life-changing. In reality, it is a big part of the reason for us even having great inner health. Of course, that is for us personally. It is for our well-being and for the benefit of those who live closely around us, who interact with us. But there is another spectacular dimension to our pursuit of thriving inner health, that makes it all worth it on another level. Discovering this is what I call "finding your value." Join me there in my final chapter.

Chapter 18

Finding Your Value

I sincerely hope it has been helpful for you, tracking with me as I shared my journey of discovery into inner health and wholeness. There have certainly been some deep concepts to consider. I hope you have been excited to engage some new techniques, learn some new disciplines, and even discover new things about yourself. The opportunities we have in the new creation are profound, and I really do hope you are on board with pursuing those too. I will be happy if you feel you are more on the pathway to freedom and wholeness, even experiencing a reset in your inner self. It will all have been so worth it.

But in this closing chapter, I need to just make one final pivot. Although it is extremely worthwhile for each and every one of us to enjoy more personal freedom and wholeness, it would be remiss of me to leave it there. Because there is an even more wonderful end in view in the new creation. It is not just about us becoming a new creation as individuals. Much more, it is about us being part of a new creation race. It is more about "we" than it is about "me."

In the new creation, there is something more dynamic than you and me just doing well. Of course, that is completely valid and very important. Every one of us has great value. Never let anyone tell you otherwise. Not only did God love us first, but He acted on it. He made a way for us to come into wholeness, and He welcomed us into His love.

But He had an even greater end in mind than that, a spectacular purpose that might come as a very big surprise to some.

He wanted to create a bride for His Son, for Jesus.

The whole Bible is really an unfolding story of God's purpose in creating a bride for Jesus. It begins with the creation account, where He made man in His image and then produced a bride for him, and it ends with the marriage of Jesus and His bride.

In the creation of man, there was no suitable partner for the man God had made. The only way God could get a compatible bride for the man was by putting him to sleep and taking a rib from his side. He then formed the rib into the woman—his bride.[181] Similarly, it would appear that God could not find a compatible bride for Jesus, either. As He looked around the eternal universe, it seems there was none compatible. So in similar fashion, He put Jesus to sleep, to take a rib from His side.

The sleep for Jesus was His physical death on the cross. His death was not eternal death, just physical, and He rose again. But on the way, while His body hung there physically dead, they pierced His side: "One of the soldiers pierced His side with a spear, and immediately blood and water came out."[182]

What was the blood and water? It was His rib (allegorically speaking). His bride came from His side. The blood and water were to become fashioned into His bride.

Let me try to explain this. In his first letter, John says, "Who is the one who overcomes the world, but he who believes that Jesus is the Son of God? This is the One who came by *water* and *blood*, Jesus Christ; not with the water only, but with the water and with the blood. It is the Spirit who testifies, because the Spirit is the truth. For there are three that testify: the *Spirit* and the *water* and the *blood*; and the three are in agreement"[183] (emphasis mine).

We know that the new creation emerged through the action of the Holy Spirit, but here it specifically mentions the water and the blood also. The new creation emerged "from His side" because that is where the water and blood emerged from. When we are recreated with our new spirit, this is by the Holy Spirit, but also seemingly by water too.[184] The water is described elsewhere in the Bible as the "Word,"[185] the seed that causes the new spiritual birth to actually happen.[186] As for the blood, in addition to this creation by the water of the Word, it was the blood of Jesus that sealed the new covenant, assigning the victory of the

---

[181] Genesis 2:20–24.
[182] John 19:34.
[183] 1 John 5:5–8.
[184] John 3:5.
[185] Ephesians 5:26.
[186] 1 Peter 1:23.

cross to all who believe. At the Last Supper, Jesus said, "For this is My blood of the covenant, which is poured out for many for forgiveness of sins."[187] So it was His blood that opened the way into freedom. The blood and water are the basis of the new creation race.

All who experience the new birth are the new creation, which the Bible collectively calls "the church." This is not a reference to a physical institution or religious organization. It is all those who have transferred out of the fallen and dark creation and into the new creation in God's love and light.[188] This new creation people are the special people formed for Jesus's own possession[189], His very own "bride".

In a remarkable passage in Ephesians, Paul unfolds the revelation that this "church" is indeed the "Bride of Christ." Follow with me through this series of verses:

"Christ also loved the *church* and gave Himself up for her, so that He might sanctify her, having cleansed her by the washing of water with the word, that He might present to Himself the church in all her glory, having no spot or wrinkle or any such thing; but that she would be holy and blameless."[190] (emphasis mine).

Paul then went on to quote the original Genesis account written first about Adam and Eve:

"For this reason a man shall leave his father and mother and shall be joined to his wife, and the two shall become one flesh."[191]

He then made this incredible statement:

"This mystery is great; but I am speaking with reference to Christ and the church."[192]

The church is the bride of Christ! This body of people, the new creation race, are created together, "spotless, holy, and blameless": perfect and pure as Jesus's bride. They have been made one together, and the purity in the new

---

[187] Matthew 26:28.

[188] 1 Peter 2:9, Colossians 1:12–13.

[189] Titus 2:11–14.

[190] Ephesians 5:25–27.

[191] Ephesians 5:31, Genesis 2:24.

[192] Ephesians 5:32.

creation spirit is what makes them compatible. We can never add to that purity, and neither will it ever corrupt itself. This is remarkable.

But how then are we to live? How are we to behave as His bride?

This is pretty sobering and a lot more than we can probably get our minds around. It will take the rest of forever to discover all that it means. But I want to suggest just three immediate and practical priorities.

First, engaging a bridal identity should draw us into a devoted lifestyle, seeking ever-growing closeness in our personal relationship with Jesus. He showed such immense love when He paid the agonizing price for our freedom. Recognizing this fuels a response of heartfelt worship. The more we engage and make worship a lifestyle, the more we flourish in intimacy with Him.

Second, discovering our inclusion in Jesus's bride should motivate us to pursue full freedom and wholeness as we have been discussing throughout this book, because full freedom and wholeness equates with full purity. Our pursuit of purity is part of our worship response. We should have desires not just to be pure by virtue of the fact that our new spirit is pure, but also to actually outwork purity as a lifestyle. It is a bridal calling.

Third, by definition, we cannot live this out alone. We are not so much the bride of Christ individually, but together. Together, we are His body. We only experience fulfilment as being part of the bride, when engaging with others in the new creation. Accordingly, we should willingly and enthusiastically take our place in the bride, to actively bring who we are, to contribute our value.

We have all been recreated with unique and specific embedded gifts and callings, and we are each to bring those and flow together in them as one body. Then we can become more completely all we are meant to be, both as individuals, and together: "But speaking the truth in love, we are to grow up in all aspects into Him who is the head, even Christ, from whom the whole body, being fitted and held together by what every joint supplies, according to the proper working of each individual part, causes the growth of the body for the building up of itself in love."[193]

"Just as we have many members in one body and all the members do not have the same function, so we, who are many, are one body in Christ, and individually members one of another. Since we have gifts that differ according to the grace given to us, each of us is to exercise them accordingly."[194]

We find true and full expression of our value, and who we really are, in this bigger picture. In the new creation, we are all called to find our place in the body, the bride. Each and every one of us has immense value and a real part to play. Can you see now how vital it is that we learn to walk out all we have become in the new creation? If we don't, all we can bring is the mixture of old and new, still struggling along in inner disharmony. But as we engage and pursue full freedom, as we have been learning through this book, we can take our place fully in His glorious bride. We can become part of God's purpose that He set in motion before the world began.[195]

From my experience, finding a new creation community that understands and pursues this well can be a challenge. There is a lot of mixture and confusion. But I wonder if you personally can feel a desire, a hope, an excitement even, rising up within yourself, to discover this kind of experience, and actually live in it with others? My ultimate hope in sharing my story, and my unfolding discovery and breakthrough, is that it might open your eyes to see this stunning potential.

If this journey together has opened up a new sense of identity, purpose, and value to you, I wonder if you might be open to sharing it with others? If so, you may soon find yourself part of a flourishing small group, where you can explore and enjoy this wonderful new creation reality together. You could maybe even get started with a group

---

[193] Ephesians 4:15–16.

[194] Romans 12:4–6.

[195] Ephesians 1:4, 2 Timothy 1:9.

by doing a study together on this book. Once formed, you could explore how God might invite you to participate with Him together, as He continues to expand His kingdom on the earth.[196]

Whatever course you follow from here, though, may you absolutely flourish and blossom into all you were created to be.

This has been a relatively brief book. In some ways, it is foundational, providing a basis for us to build from. I am actively working on other materials too, that might help further. If that is of interest, or you would like to keep up to date with what is happening on that front, please check out my website at newcreationlife.net.

"Beloved, I pray that in all respects you may prosper and be in good health, just as your soul prospers."[197]

Abundant blessings!

---

[196] Isaiah 9:7.
[197] 3 John 2.

Epilogue: The Big Questions Finally Answered

If you have reached this far, well done. We have come a long, long way together.

When you started reading this book, you might never have imagined that this is where it would end. Perhaps it has radically reset who you are, how you live, and your inner motivations and expectations, your inner beliefs. Or at least you have got to thinking more that way, more determined on your pathway of discovery. Hopefully, you can see that you have wide-reaching opportunity to change, flourishing in freedom, and growing more and more into the wholeness that is available in the new creation.

Although the leopard cannot change its spots, we are more than leopards. We truly can reset our inner self.

Now, for a closing thought, and to summarize all this again in terms of our ultimate purpose and destiny, I want to quote from an unlikely source. This is not a new idea.

Many years ago, a group of Christian leaders met together at what is known as the "Westminster Catechism" in London. Way back in 1646, in fact. After much study, discussion, and reflection, they reached a conclusion on what they called "the chief end of man" (humankind).

This is the ultimate answer to some of the biggest questions in humanity.

> Why am I here? Why do I exist? What is my purpose?

And, of course …

Why are *we* here? Why do *we* exist? What is *our* purpose?

After nearly four hundred years, I am not sure we could improve on their conclusion very much:

"Man's chief end is to glorify God and to enjoy him for ever."[xviii]

Here is destiny, purpose, and focus. Living in anything less, any watered-down version, is not true freedom or wholeness. God bless you, as you flourish into all that exists in His new creation potential, glorifying God and enjoying Him fully, both in this life and on into eternity.

MEET KAINOS[1]
"THE NEW[1] CREATION PERSON"

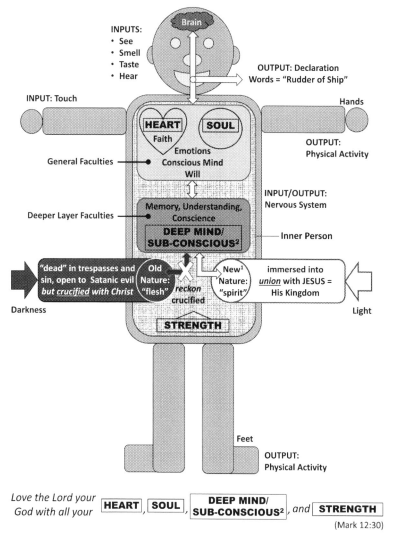

Love the Lord your God with all your **HEART**, **SOUL**, **DEEP MIND/ SUB-CONSCIOUS[2]**, *and* **STRENGTH**

(Mark 12:30)

if anyone is in Christ, he is a new[1] creature; the old things passed away; behold, new things have come. (2 Corinthians 5:17)

[1] Greek kainos = "new (of a different kind)"
[2] Greek dianoia = "deep mind, second part"

Special Section: The Love Cycle

In chapter 14, I explained that our engagement with our subconscious deepens our experience of relationship with God. We develop our relationship with Him the more we learn to walk in the new creation life. In chapter 16, we discovered that we activate the new creation life by faith, and this is specifically faith in "the Son of God who loved us."[198] In fact, Paul said that "faith working through love" is what matters.[199] Everything in the new creation life operates in God's love.

In addition, the primary response God is looking for from us is to love Him back. Loving Him back is the "greatest commandment," where I first discovered the revelation of the subconscious in the Bible (see chapter 12): "You shall love the Lord your God with all your heart, all your soul, all your mind [subconscious], and all your strength."[200]

The more I contemplated this, the more I began to realize that this works like a *cycle* of love. God loving me, me loving Him back. This is incredibly powerful and can motivate us in everything we have been discussing in this book. We can be energized by love. Never underestimate the power of God's love.

One evening, during the Covid-19 pandemic, we had a new creation small-group gathering at our home (we were not under isolation mandates at this point in time). One of

---

[198] Galatians 2:20.
[199] Galatians 5:6.
[200] Mark 12:30.

the young women present was deeply troubled because her father, who was living in another state, had developed extremely serious Covid-19 symptoms and looked close to death. It was unclear if he would survive even the rest of that night. We began to pray for her and then her dad. Another group member had earlier shared how that morning she had been freshly struck by the power of God's love. Suddenly, in the middle of our group prayer time, she loudly and powerfully proclaimed the words, "The love of God!" There was immediately a tangible presence of God in the room. All other prayers stopped. We just sat, consumed by His awesomeness. That night, nearly eighteen hundred miles away, our friend's dad made a sudden, dramatic recovery, was able to leave the hospital soon after, and was restored to full health. The medical professionals in attendance were perplexed, as well as deeply relieved. The pandemic was at its height in that location, and they were only too familiar with its power to kill.

I share this just as an example, rather than making any suggestion that this is some special formula for physical healing. But from that time, I have been even more impacted by the potential power in the love of God.

Paul says, "But in all these things we overwhelmingly conquer through Him who loved us. For I am convinced that neither death, nor life, nor angels, nor principalities, nor things present, nor things to come, nor powers, nor height, nor depth, nor any other created thing, will be able to separate us from the love of God, which is in Christ Jesus our Lord."[201]

Let me explain how the love cycle works. This is the culture in which the new creation life flourishes.

First, let us realize that God's decision to bring a solution to a fallen and corrupt human race was motivated by His love. It all started with Him. This is from the famous John 3:16 verse: "For God so loved the world, that He gave His only begotten Son..."

Taking this a step further, John proclaimed that "God

---

[201] Romans 8:37–39.

is love."[202] God doesn't just have love, He is love. When He enters our life in the new creation act of forming our new spirit, we encounter this love. John went on to say, "He loved us first," and this is what allows us to love also. God's love is the reason, the basis, and the enabling power for us to love.

"We love, because He first loved us."[203]

As I mentioned above, we know that the greatest commandment is that we love God back, literally with everything we have: with our heart, soul, mind (subconscious), and strength. The second commandment expands this to also "loving our neighbor as ourselves."[204] By design, we are energized and empowered into fulfilment of those major commandments, as we first receive God's love ourselves. That is the key. But then John makes it clear that a primary focus is for us to also extend this love to specifically loving others in the new creation family. He said, "The one who loves God should love *his brother* also"[205] (emphasis mine).

Jesus announced this as a new commandment: "A new commandment I give to you, that you love one another, even as I have loved you, that you also love one another. By this all men will know that you are My disciples, if you have love for one another."[206]

Can you see what God is creating in the new creation? A community of love. I explained that ultimate purpose in my final chapter. Our place as the bride of Christ is founded in love.

Regarding my idea of a love cycle, Jesus outlined a spiritual law that unleashes incredible power. It is the law of giving and receiving, where Jesus said, "Give, and it will be given to you. They will pour into your lap a good measure—pressed down, shaken together, and running over. For by

---

[202] 1 John 4:8.
[203] 1 John 4:19.
[204] Mark 12:31.
[205] 1 John 4:21.
[206] John 13:34–35.

your standard of measure it will be measured to you in return."[207]

So I must ask you: How big was God's measure of love towards us? He loved us first. He is love, so my guess is that was huge. Now, if we engage the spiritual law of giving and receiving, it will be set in motion within us. We will find His great love, with which He loves us, emerging out from within us back to Him. First He gave, and so now He will receive back. But now, we have become the giver. Do you see that? And do you know what happens next? Now that we have given love, the law of giving and receiving kicks in and causes love to be given back to us again, pressed down, shaken together, running over. This is the love cycle.

Becoming established in this, we now have something remarkable to bring into community, as we also extend this love to others. In one sense, we are just loving others by loving God. John said, "We love the children of God, when we love God."[208] This is how we love even those we might

207 Luke 6:38.
208 1 John 5:2.

struggle to love in the natural. It is supernatural. It is the new creation.

We will do well to make sure that we keep this love cycle working within us and through us. If it feels blocked in you, I found that you can reactivate it by engaging in one of two ways (or both). First, focus on the fact that you received God's love already, and engage with that. Use the intentional calmness and visualization techniques we learned. Maybe use this verse: "The love of God has been poured out within our hearts through the Holy Spirit who was given to us."[209]

Visualize God's love as a warm balm, flooding through your heart. As you do that, the truth and reality of His love within you can start to flow again.

The second way to reactivate the love cycle is to decide to actively express love to God, maybe by using a worship song or prayer of gratitude. Or you could love God by intentionally loving a brother or sister. Any or all of these will kick-start the love cycle again. And once it is running freely, it will keep refueling itself. Receive and give, give and receive.

The love cycle floods us with a new inner harmony, which enables the new creation life to fully manifest and flourish.

In the love of God, every sense of blandness is gone. So is every other negative symptom we identified in our diagnostic check-up, back in chapter 3: hopelessness, or being dissatisfied, loneliness, inadequacy or inferiority, inner anger, antagonism, and indecisiveness. All gone! Irrational fears and panic attacks, overthrown![210] God's love, energizing the new creation reality, triumphs over all. Death is "swallowed up in victory".[211]

Now, we arrive in a place of settled joy, just like Jesus said He wanted for us: "These things I have spoken to you

---

[209] Romans 5:5.

[210] 1 John 4:18.

[211] 1 Corinthians 15:54.

so that My joy may be in you, and that your joy may be made full."[212]

The love cycle is powerful. This is the energy for our complete, sustainable, inner health.

---
[212] John 15:11.

Image Attributions

Book cover
https://pixabay.com/illustrations/leopard-look-wild-art-watercolor-3537408/

Free for commercial use. Thank you, Ractapopulous, for sharing this stunning picture and allowing its use!

Chapter 1: Car
Sketch by author, all rights reserved

Chapter 2: Map route
Sketch by author, all rights reserved

Chapter 3: Stethoscope
Sketch by author, all rights reserved

Chapter 4: Calm scene
Jean-Antoine-Théodore de Gudin, Riverscape with Boats

The Walters Art Museum, creative commons: https://art.thewalters.org/detail/39358/riverscape-with-boats/

Chapter 5: Visualize
Francesco Vanni, Head of a Man with Closed Eyes

The Met Museum, public domain: https://www.metmuseum.org/art/collection/search/340927

Chapter 6: Broken heart

Chapter 7: Iceberg

Chapter 8: U-Turn

Chapter 9: Cows
Thomas Rowlandson, Three Cows Standing on the Ridge of a Field

Chapter 10: Building ruin
Chapman, J.G. (John Gadsby), The American drawing-book: a manual for the amateur, and basis of study for the professional artist : especially adapted to the use of public and private schools, as well as home instruction

Chapter 11: Gift Box

Chapter 12: Bible

Chapter 13: Gears

14: Rose
F.E. Pease, Pease Garden and Nursery

Chapter 15: Talking head
Mohamed Hassan

Chapter 16: Cross and heart

Chapter 17: Ship
William Daniell, Three Masted Ship

Chapter 18: Community

Kainos

The Love Cycle: Cyclical Arrows

About the Author

Michael J. Parkyn was born in England, where he grew up and qualified as a construction management professional. At the age of twenty three, he had a sudden, unexpected spiritual awakening at an inspirational rock concert in London, which propelled him on to a whole new direction in his life.

Gripped with the pursuit of discovering all that this new life entailed, he engaged in pastoral and missions work, including being based intentionally for different periods of time on all four continents either side of the Atlantic (Europe, Africa, and North and South America). Work assignments also took him to Australia and Asia, and he served as a local church pastor for over two years as close as you can live as a nonscientist to Antarctica (The Falkland Islands). He counts it a privilege to have touched (almost) all seven continents.

In 2005, after nearly twenty years in missions and full-time ministry assignments, Michael re-entered the professional marketplace. From that place of integration with people of varied beliefs, values, and cultures, he was able to grow more in understanding and serve as a volunteer leader, especially through inspirational small groups.

Michael has worked as a regional director, operations manager, pastor, and quantity surveyor, while also leading countless ministry expressions and forging purposeful and impactful mentoring relationships. Through all of this, he has been exposed to many of the challenges different people face in life and has held out a vision for bringing growth and positive change to many. Ordained to international church planting and leadership with Church of the Nations[xix] in 1991, Michael also became a certified team member of Maxwell Leadership (John C. Maxwell)[xx] in 2020.

After more than thirty years growing in understanding of his Bible-based faith, Michael discovered life-changing insight to the working of the subconscious realm. Tying the spiritual and psychological together opened the pathway to significant personal breakthrough and growth, opening greater understanding and momentum for building lives and bringing positive change.

Michael married Heather in South Africa in 1988, and they now live in Kansas City, Missouri, in the United States. At the time of writing, they have four children and six grandchildren.

Endnotes

i   Collins Dictionary online, https://www.collinsdictionary.com/us/dictionary/english/a-leopard-cannot-change-its-spots

ii   Maltz, Maxwell, *Psycho Cybernetics* (New York: Tarcher Perigee, 2015)

iii   Strong's Dictionary G2942, https://www.blueletterbible.org/

iv   Maltz, *Psycho Cybernetics*

v   Britannica.com   https://www.britannica.com/technology/servomechanism

vi   Science Direct online, https://www.sciencedirect.com/topics/engineering/servomechanism

vii   https://www.guinnessworldrecords.com/world-records/best-selling-book-of-non-fiction

viii   Richard Weissbourd, Milena Batanova, Virginia Lovison, and Eric Torres, *Loneliness in America: How the Pandemic Has Deepened an Epidemic of Loneliness and What We Can Do About It*

ix   https://www. quotefancy.com/quote/799618

x   https://www.who.int/data/gho/data/major-themes/health-and-well-being

xi   Roland A. Vandell, Robert. A. Davis, and Herbert A. Clugston, "The function of mental practice in the acquisition of motor skills." *Journal of General Psychology* 29, 243–250. https://doi.org/10.1080/00221309.1943.10544442

xii   A. J. Adams, MAPP, Psychology Today; Seeing Is Believing: The Power of Visualization. Posted December 3, 2009 https://www.psychologytoday.com/us/blog/flourish/200912/seeing-is-believing-the-power-visualization, viewed 09/08/2022

xiii   Adams, Psychology Today; Seeing Is Believing: The Power of Visualization

xiv Alan Richardson, "Mental Practice: A Review and Discussion Part I," *Research Quarterly* (American Association for Health, Physical Education and Recreation), 38:1, 1967, 95–107, DOI: 10.1080/10671188.1967.10614808

xv   Adams, Psychology Today; Seeing Is Believing: The Power of Visualization

xvi Richardson, Mental Practice

xvii Justin Welby in his address at the funeral of Queen Elizabeth II, London, England, 09/19/2022

xviii https://prts.edu/wp-content/uploads/2016/12/Shorter_Catechism.pdf retrieved 09/09/2022

xix https://cotn.org/

xx   https://www.maxwellleadership.com/

Printed in the United States
by Baker & Taylor Publisher Services